C. Struik (Pty) Ltd
Oswald Pirow Street, Foreshore
Cape Town 8001

Reg. no. 80/02842/07

First published – 1981
Revised edition – 1982
Second impression – 1984
Revised edition – 1985
Second impression – 1986
Third impression – 1987
Printed and bound by
National Book Printers, Goodwood
© Clive Walker

ISBN 0 86977 260 0

SIGNS
of the
WILD

Field Guide to the Spoor and Signs of the Mammals of Southern Africa

Clive Walker

C. STRUIK PUBLISHERS, CAPE TOWN

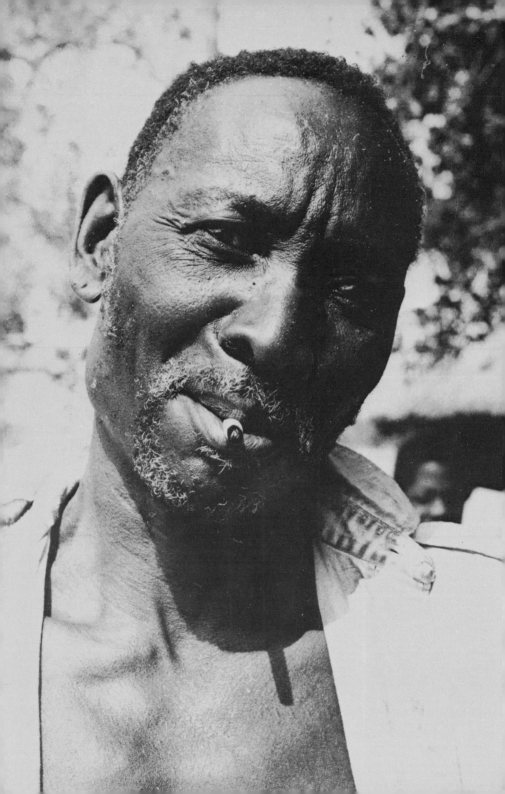

CONTENTS

Preamble... 8
Acknowledgements.. 12
Environmental Glossary... 14

Mammal Index:

Erinaceidae — Hedgehog 18

Galagidae — Night Ape 19
— Bushbaby....................................... 20

Cercopithecidae — Vervet Monkey 23
— Samango Monkey 25
— Chacma Baboon.......................... 27

Manidae — Pangolin 29

Leporidae — Hares 30

Sciuridae — Squirrels 32

Pedetidae — Springhare 36

Thryonomidae — Greater Cane Rat........................ 37

Hystricidae — Porcupine 41

Canidae — Cape Hunting Dog........................ 45
— Cape Fox.................................... 49
— Bat-eared Fox 53
— Black-backed Jackal.................... 57
— Side-striped Jackal...................... 61

Mustelidae — Striped Polecat............................. 64
— Striped Weasel 65
— Honeybadger 67
— Spotted-necked Otter.................. 69
— Clawless Otter............................ 71

Viverridae — Civet 73
— Genets... 75
— Suricate 77
— Meller's Mongoose...................... 78
— Yellow Mongoose......................... 79
— Selous' Mongoose 80
— Cape Grey Mongoose 81
— Water Mongoose......................... 82
— White-tailed Mongoose 83
— Large Grey Mongoose................. 84
— Slender Mongoose....................... 85
— Banded Mongoose 86
— Dwarf Mongoose 87

Hyaenidae — Aardwolf 89
— Spotted Hyaena 91
— Brown Hyaena 95

Felidae — Lion 97
— Leopard 101
— Cheetah 105
— Caracal 105
— Serval 111
— Wild Cat 112
— Black-footed Cat 113

Orycteropidae — Antbear 115

Elephantidae — Elephant 117

Procaviidae — Tree Dassie 124
— Rock Dassie 125
— Yellow-spotted Dassie 126
— Kaokoveld Rock Dassie 127

Rhinocerotidae — Black Rhinoceros 129
— White Rhinoceros 133

Equidae — Burchell's Zebra 137
— Mountain Zebra 141

Suidae — Bush Pig 145
— Warthog 149

Hippopotamidae — Hippopotamus 153

Giraffidae — Giraffe 161

Bovidae — Damara Dik-dik 162
— Oribi 163
— Suni 164
— Grysbok 165
— Sharpe's Grysbok 167
— Grey Rhebuck 168
— Klipspringer 169
— Blue Duiker 170
— Red Forest Duiker 171
— Grey Duiker 172
— Steenbok 173
— Blesbok 175
— Bontebok 177
— Reedbuck 179
— Mountain Reedbuck 181
— Springbok 183
— Impala 185
— Blue Wildebeest 187

— Black Wildebeest................189
— Tsessebe 191
— Gemsbok 193
— Red Hartebeest 195
— Sable Antelope...................197
— Roan Antelope....................201
— Puku 203
— Waterbuck..........................205
— Red Lechwe 207
— Bushbuck...........................209
— Nyala.................................211
— Sitatunga...........................213
— Kudu 215
— Eland.................................217
— Buffalo...............................219

Comparative Spoor Illustrations 220
Author's Notes 227
Bibliography 228
Index... 230

Preamble

"They hear on the wind, as it passes, the call of the veld"
Mary Byron, "The Call of the Veld"

Years ago as a very young man hunting elephants in the Mahell area, near the Olifants river in Mocambique, I first learnt what wind meant when crawling on all fours — the heavy .416 calibre rifle feeling like some large chunk of lead and not the finely engineered instrument of destruction it was.

We knew they were ahead, because we could hear the tearing of branches and the rumbling, so well known with these giants. I was a complete novice in the art of stalking and well aware of the acute senses of these creatures with which we sought to close, and the wind, which is all important in their struggle with man.

The heat, humidity and closeness of that thick bush was unbelievable and suddenly, silence — not even, it seemed, the song of birds — just nothing . . . those who have stalked elephant, will understand exactly what I mean . . . the silence prolonged and the suspense considerable.

I remember looking at Hans Bufe, wanting him to make the decision, but he did not have to, for they were gone — on the wind . . . The wind, which plays such an important part in the bushveld. Get to know it, and you can make it work for you, but it can just as easily work against you.

The game trails are being followed more and more by those in pursuit of understanding the signs of the wild and less and less by those in the wake of the gun.

The bushveld is not always the scene of vast numbers of moving animals, but more often empty and silent except, perhaps, for the wind. All around us, however, we find the signs of the passing of many species of wildlife — a honey badger, seldom seen, who passed this way during the night. How do we know it passed in the night? Do we know its spoor or its faeces or do we find a portion of honey comb or, possibly, a hole reaching down nearly 60 cm with dark brown, sweet tasting honey at the bottom? These are some of the questions I have often asked myself.

The hunter-gatherers knew — for it is the source of life. Men such as Selous, Finaughty, Petrus Jacobs and Viljoen knew, for it was part of their profession. Rangers, trackers and scouts know. The black man, in particular, knows for he grew up with it. But what of the new band of scientists, naturalists, trailers and ordinary men and women, boys and girls who seek to understand more of the ways of the wild?

Driving along a dusty track in Sabie-Sand during 1974, we stopped to observe tracks in the fine sand and it was interesting how many ventured different interpretations of what animal had passed. It was here that I determined to study "signs". At that time, it seemed that spoor was the most important, but that is only one aspect of many. Later, Professor Bothma of Pretoria University felt there was a need for a study on faeces (dung) and advised me to pursue all and every sign.

Collecting dung is not without its moments of amusement and most people are faintly puzzled when they observe you picking up animal droppings and placing them in little plastic bags.

The project was initiated in July 1974. The study area was Africa south of the Kunene and Zambesi Rivers and incorporated aspects of spoor (footprints) and signs (feeding, faeces — droppings), markings and shelters or homes of the mammals of southern Africa, the smallest being the tree squirrel. Apart from the squirrels, springhares, cane rats and the porcupines; the rodentia, chiroptera (bats) and insectivora have been excluded.

In certain instances, I have relied on other people's assistance, for although I have travelled through many parts of southern Africa, I have at times had to rely on observations by others. I must state at the outset that our basic knowledge of much of what we have acquired in our understanding of this subject has been passed on by the black man. He has grown up to understand these things as a matter of course and one can only gain from his experience.

Acknowledgements

It is impossible to write a book of this nature without the assistance of many people. Our knowledge of environmental awarenes is a continuing process and in the words of Dave Rushworth: "If we are to be selfish in our knowledge, we cannot hope to teach conservation".

I should like to express my gratitude to all who have helped, in particular: Prof. J. du P. Bothma, Eugène Marais Chair of Wildlife Management, University of Pretoria, for the facilities he placed at my disposal and for checking the script.

Prof. F.C. Eloff, Head, Department of Zoology, University of Pretoria, with whom I had the great pleasure of working in the Kalahari Gemsbok National Park whilst studying the Kalahari lion, and later, in Kaokoland on elephants. This gave me a rare opportunity to gain first hand information on the desert fauna.

Johannes Naari and Johannes Phetoue of Botswana, with whom I have worked and shared many experiences. It was they who, more than any one else I know taught me the ways of the wild and of elephants. Shamwari from Stabatswane.

The Bushman trackers in the Kalahari — 'Tokolosh', Tsipan and 'Houthoop' — the like of their endurance I had never seen before and their observations of desert life were of immense value.

Tom Moiiamudi, the game guard of Giraffe Game Reserve.

Winnis Watebula from Sabie-Sand Wildtuin — he started out in life as a herdboy with the renowned Harry Kirkman. When Kirkman joined Stevenson-Hamilton in 1924, he tended Stevenson-Hamilton's cattle and then became a game guard under the late Harold Trollope.

The Zulu Game Guards and, in particular, Johannes of the Umfolozi Game Reserve. There are many of us who learnt from these men.

Dhalamini — the Lake St. Lucia Game Guard.

Mokabela — a guide in the Okavango.

The list is long, from Mocambique in the east to the Namib in the west. The pages of this book are full of their knowledge.

The Transvaal Division of Nature Conservation; the Department of Wildlife and National Parks, Botswana, the Natal Parks Board.

Jim Feely, Neville Peake, Bob Lawrence, John Varty, Harry Millar, Malcolm Simpson, Michael Brett and, particularly, Don Richards — my co-author of "Walk Through the Wilderness" — men who love the bush and who have been most helpful.

Prof. G.K. Theron of the Department of Botany, University of Pretoria.

Prof. John Skinner and his students at the Mammal Research Institute, University of Pretoria. In particular, San Viljoen and Johan Bester.

Mr. Willie Labuschagne, Johannesburg Zoological Gardens.

Dr. Woody Meltzer and Eugene Marais. Lloyd Wilmot of Botswana.

David Rowe-Rowe for information on otters, and Nicole Duplaix of the New York Zoological Society.

Peter Hitchins for information on the black rhinoceros.

Charles Norman, Larry Patterson and Paul Zway.

Dr. Reay Smithers for spoor and distribution advice.

Mark Berry for work on the bat-eared fox.

Val Ford who typed the manuscript.

To my wife, Conita, who has encouraged and assited me both in the field and at home and, not forgetting my sons, Renning and Anton. In particular, Renning, who acquired his own collection and takes such an interest in natural history.

There comes a time in everyone's life when you are fortunate enough to make friends with one of nature's true gentlemen, the late Hans Bufe, "Home from the Hills". When I was barely out of school, I faced an African elephant on foot at 5 metres in the Mocambique bush by the side of this man. A hunter of immense skill, I learnt from him that bushcraft is not picked up in a day. He was a legend in his lifetime and I owe my start in wildlife to him.

I wish to acknowledge with appreciation the assistance rendered in this revised edition: Libby Parker, Sandi Eastwood, Koos Bothma, Suzy Ellis and Ted Reilly of Mlilwane Wildlife Sanctuary.

Environmental Glossary

Adaptation:
The ability, through inherited structural or functional characteristics, that improves the survival rate of animal or plant in a particular habitat.

Arboreal:
Living in trees.

Bacteria:
Single-celled microscopic organisms found in every habitat, ecosystem or cycle.

Carnivore:
An animal that lives by eating the flesh of other animals.

Carrion:
Dead and decaying flesh of animals.

Commensalism:
A relationship between two organisms in which one partner is helped and the other is neither helped nor harmed, that is, two organisms existing in the same habitat.

Conservation:
The wise use of the earth's natural resources that ensures their continuing availability for generations to come.

Diurnal:
Active by day.

Drought:
An indefinite period of time when little or no rain falls on an area.

Ecology:
The study of the relationships of living things to each other and to their non-living environment.

Environment:
The term which describes all external conditions such as soil, water, air and organisms, surrounding a living thing.

Erosion:
The weathering of the earth's surface by water, wind, ice and other natural forces.

Faeces (droppings):
Residue of indigestible food. Secretions and bacteria passed from the alimentary canal through the anus.

Gregarious:
Living in communities.

Grazer:
An animal that feeds on grass, such as a zebra or some antelopes.

Habitat:
The immediate surroundings of a plant or animal which has everything necessary to life in a particular area.

Herbivore:
An animal that utilises plants as food.

Mammals:
The term for that group of animals including humans, bats, cattle etc, — which are all warm-blooded, have milk-producing glands, are partially covered with hair and normally bear their young alive.

Melapo:
A flooded grass plain.

Mutualism:
A relationship between two organisms in which both partners benefit from the relationship.

Nocturnal:
Active at night.

Overgrazing:
Intensive feeding on the vegetation of an area by wild or domestic animals which causes serious and often permanent damage to the area's plant life.

Omnivorous:
Feeding on anything available.

Predator:
An animal that lives by capturing other animals for food.

Prey:
A living animal that is captured by a predator such as a lion, leopard or cheetah for food.

Pride:
A family or group of lions.

Scavenger:
An animal like the vulture or hyaena that lives by devouring the dead remains of other animals and plants.

Shrub:
A small woody plant with more than one stem rising from the ground.

Species:
The term is singular or plural, and relates to a group of plants or animals with common characteristics.

Spoor:
From the Dutch word meaning footprint. Track or trail.

Symbiosis:
An association of two different organisms in a relationship that may benefit one or both partners. For example in the case of the symbiotic relationship called parasitism, one partner (the parasite) benefits and the other partner (the host) is harmed by the association.

Terrestrial:
Living on the land.

Territory:
An animal's domain which he defends against members of his own species or other species.

Veld:
A local term for open land used for grazing and other needs.

SIGNS
of the
WILD

Hedgehog
Krimpvarkie
(Erinaceus frontalis)

Shona: Shoni **Ndebele:** Inhloni **Zulu:** Nhloni
Siswati: Nduundvunduwane **Venda:** Tshitoni
Tswana; Sotho: Thlong

Diet:
Omnivorous; termites, insects, millipedes, centipedes, snails, frogs, lizards, small rodents, young birds, eggs, wild fruits and various vegetable matter.

General:
Mainly nocturnal, found singly, in pairs or in family groups. Good sense of smell. Hides up in a variety of vegetation, in holes or amongst rocks. Very inactive during the winter months.

Actual Size

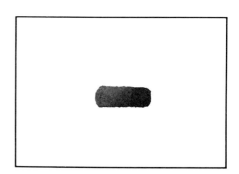

Description:
Overall length: 20 cm
Mass: 0,4 kg
Gestation: 40 days

Spoor:
1,5–2 cm, four-clawed toes
(After Smithers).

Faeces:
Not collected.
Described by R. Smithers.

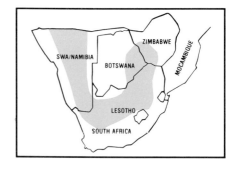

Lesser Bushbaby
Nagapie
(Galago senegalensis)

Shona: Chinhavira   **Ndebele:** Impukunyani
Shangaan: Mhimbi   **Tswana:** Mogwele
Transvaal Sotho: Maselale-ntlwë **Venda:** Tshimondi
Lozi: Bunde   **Yei:** Unqwa

Diet:
Mainly insects. Also includes flowers, fruits and *Acacia* gum.

General:
As their Afrikaans name implies, these small animals are nocturnal, occurring in pairs or singly. Widespread in distribution throughout our region. Excellent jumpers. Eyes shine brightly when a light is shone in their direction. Arboreal, they seldom come onto the ground. Nests of grass and leaves in the hollows or holes of trees. Voice is a shrill, plaintive cry.

Actual Size

O └──┴──┴──┴──┴──┘ 5 CM

Description:
Overall length: 40 cm
Mass: 0,15 kg
Gestation: 4 months, up to 3 are born.

Spoor:
3 cm long, well-rounded finger tips. Slender.

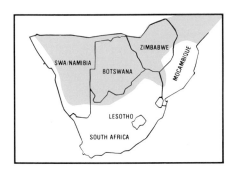

19

Thick-tailed Bushbaby Bosnagaap

(Galago crassicaudatus)

Shona: Chimhavira **Ndebele:** Impukunyoni **Zulu:** Sinkwe
Shangaan: Xidweta

Diet:
Insects, fruits, leaves, flowers, lizards, eggs and birds.

General:
Much larger animal than the lesser bushbaby, frequenting well-wooded plantations, forests, *Acacia* woodland and riverine forests. Their raucous screams can be somewhat alarming to anyone unused to them. These shrill cries probably serve as indicators of territory. They are arboreal, although they will sometimes descend to the ground. They are also nocturnal and solitary, moving silently and capable of fantastic leaps. Like the lesser bushbaby, they urinate on their feet and hands thereby marking their territories.

O └─┴─┴─┴─┴─┘ 5 CM

RS
Actual Size

Description:
Overall length: 70 cm
Mass: 1,1 kg
Gestation: 123 to 136 days

Spoor:
Like the night ape, the second toe of the hind foot has a claw for grooming.

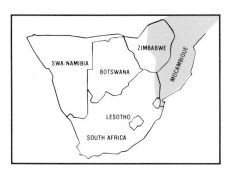

20

Their raucous screams can be most alarming to the unsuspecting wilderness trailer.

Actual Size

O | | | | | 5 CM

Vervet Monkey
Blou-aap
(Cercopithecus pygerythrus)

Shona: Tsoko/shoko **Ndebele:** Inkawu **Zulu:** Nkawu
Venda: Thobo **Tswana:** Kgatla **Siswati:** Ngobiyane
Transvaal Sotho: Kgabo
Lozi: Njoko **Yei:** Unshoko

Diet:
Omnivorous, although principally vegetarian, birds' eggs, lizards, insects, scorpions — in fact virtually anything edible. Fond of crops.

General:
Common, gregarious animals found in family troops or small parties. Found in a wide range of habitats, tree and bush savanna, montane and riverine forest to coastal bush. Not strictly arboreal, they take readily to the ground in search of food and to drink. Their senses are acute and they are constantly on the alert against predators. Predators are the leopard and the crowned eagle. Often kept as pets when young which should be avoided as they can become treacherous when older.

Description:
Overall Length: 1,2 m
Mass: males 7 kg, females 5 kg
Gestation: About 210 days.
Single young, breed throughout the year.

Spoor:
6 cm

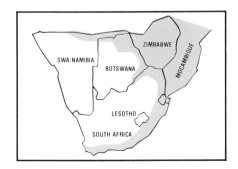

Actual Size

Samango Monkey
Samango-aap
(Cercopithecus albogularis)

Shona: Dongonda   **Ndebele:** Insimango
Xhosa, Zulu, Siswati: Nsimango   **Shangaan:** Ndlandlama   **Venda:** Dulu

Diet:
Omnivorous; fruits, vegetable matter, insects and birds' eggs.

General:
Principally arboreal, diurnal. Solitary males are often encountered, otherwise they are found in troops or family groups. Found in the eastern regions of southern Africa in the forest areas. Their range includes the Zimbabwean Eastern Highlands and into the Transvaal Klein Drakensberg, usually in high rainfall areas. Heavier than the vervet monkey and not prone to crop raiding. Preyed upon by the crowned eagle *(Stephanoaëtes coronatus).* Not as common as the vervet monkey due to a restricted range.

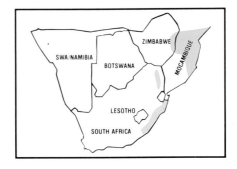

Description:
Overall Length: 1,3 m
Mass: males 9 kg, females 7 kg

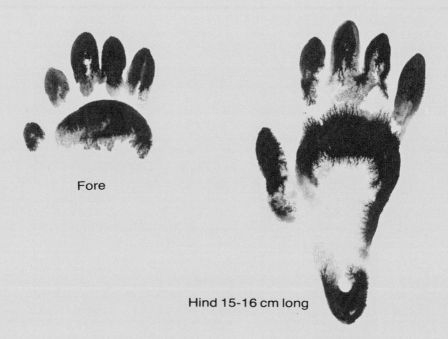

Fore

Hind 15-16 cm long

Chacma Baboon
Bobbejaan
(Papio ursinus)

Shona: Bveni, Gudo   **Ndebele:** Indwanguly   **Siswati:** mfene
Tswana: Thswene   **Venda:** Pfene   **Transvaal Sotho:** Tshwene
Lozi: Pombwe   **Yei:** Uwurutwa

Diet:
Omnivorous; fruits, leaves, tubers, roots, bulbs, scorpions — they are most adept at removing the sting from the tail, ground birds, eggs, insects, young mammals and most partial to crop raiding. The baboon will eat virtually anything.

General:
Large, powerfully built primates with a prominent dog-like muzzle and a strong jaw with canines which exceed those of a lion in length. They are terrestrial, gregarious animals and are found in small and large troops. They possess considerable intelligence and have acute eyesight and hearing. Their enemies are the leopard and man. They will often be found in the company of antelope whose additional alertness supplements their own. They frequent several sleeping sites, occupying a large tree or ledges on mountain slopes. They are noisy at dawn and dusk. Their voice is a loud, deep bark with a range of conversational utterings, shrieks and screams. Baboons have a well-developed social structure and when danger threatens, the dominant males adopt a hostile stance to protect the agile and swift troop, which rapidly disperses while the flanking members stand up in the grass or jump on to anthills or tree trunks to keep you in view. On occasions, when I have been on foot and disturbed them, my sudden presence has caused them to disappear in a free-for-all — every baboon for himself. They are fearful of leopards and will jump considerable distances in an effort to escape, all the while uttering the wildest cries.

Description:
Shoulder height: 80 cm
Mass: males 30 kg, females 18 kg
Gestation: 6 to 7 months, single young.

Spoor:
See drawing — note the largeness of the hind foot; the forefoot clearly shows the knuckles.

Faeces:
Baboons have no set pattern and their dung is found over a wide area as they move and feed. The ground under roosting spots is usually scattered with their dung.

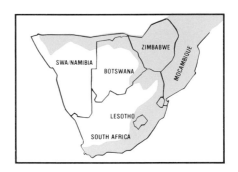

Fore

Hind

Actual Size

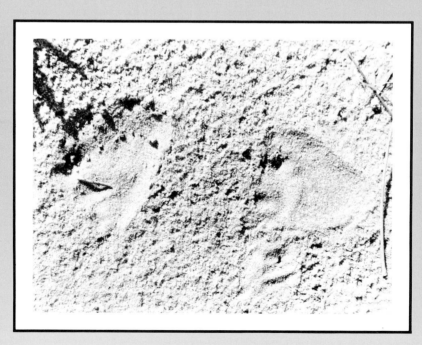

Pangolin
Ietermagog
(Manis temminckii)

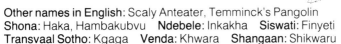

Other names in English: Scaly Anteater, Temminck's Pangolin
Shona: Haka, Hambakubvu   **Ndebele**: Inkakha   **Siswati**: Finyeti
Transvaal Sotho: Kgaga   **Venda**: Khwara   **Shangaan**: Shikwaru
Lozi: Nake   **Yei**: Unkaka

Diet:
Termites and ants. They do not possess teeth, but have instead a well-developed muscular stomach which, with the help of ingested gravel, grinds up the ants and termites.

General:
A rare, mainly nocturnal animal which lives in holes or under dense bush, curled up tightly in a ball with head and feet tucked firmly in. Moves along on its hind legs, occasionally dropping onto all fours. Highly regarded by many Africans — which may account for its rarity — for its medicinal and superstitious properties. The products are often found in 'muti' shops. Hearing extremely good.

Description:
Overall length: Up to 1 m
Mass: Up to 8 kg
Gestation: 150 days; single young.

Spoor:
The claws are prominent of which 2, 3 and 4 are well-developed and recurved. Note drawing.
Walks mainly on its hind legs in an upright position.

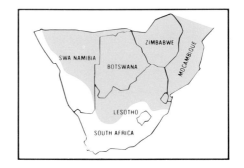

Faeces:
Not collected in the wild.

• Endangered species.

Scrub Hare
Kolhaas
(Lepus saxatilis)

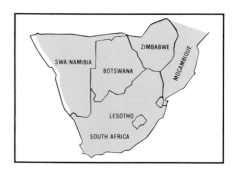

Shona: Tsuro   **Ndebele:** Umvundla   **Zulu:** Logwaja
Shangaan: Mpfundla   **Tswana:** Mutlwa   **Venda:** Muvhuda, Khomu
Southern Sotho: Mofuli   **Siswati:** Logwatja
Lozi: Shakame   **Yei:** Unshuru

Diet:
Vegetarian (grazers)

General:
Found singly and occasionally in pairs. Mainly nocturnal.
Widely distributed throughout southern Africa. Preyed upon by owls, pythons, and various Carnivora including the cheetah, who run them down.
They lie up in thick grass and under bushes. Lie with their ears flat and only dart off at the last moment. Swift, jinking run.
Have no flank stripe; more robust in build than *Lepus capensis*

Fore

Actual Size

Hind

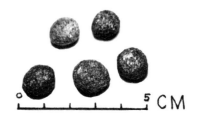

Description:
Overall Length: 40 cm
Mass: Up to 2 kg
Gestation: 30 days. Up to 2 at birth.

Spoor:
Forefoot 2 cm long, back foot
3 cm long. Note illustration.

Faeces:
Similar in all species, well
rounded, 1 cm diameter.

Cape Hare
Vlakhaas
(Lepus capensis)

Other names: As for the scrub hare
Diet: Vegetarian

General:
Slightly lighter in mass and more fragile-looking than the scrub hare and found in more open habitat. Has a clearly defined buffy flank stripe, which is less obvious in arid areas.

Red Rock Rabbits
Rooiklipkonyne
(Pronolagus species)

Siswati: Intsenetja

According to T.J. Robinson (pers. comm.) three species of red rock rabbit occur in southern Africa, viz: *P. crassicaudatus, P. rupestris* and *P. randensis.*

Diet:
Vegetarian, mainly grass.

General:
Overall colour is a darkish grey; the distinguishing features are the reddish tail and legs. Nocturnal and as the name implies, their habitat is amongst rocky hills and outcrops. The red rock rabbit does not burrow. Fleet-footed. Deposit their droppings in communal middens not unlike the rock dassie.

Description:
Overall length: 40 cm
Mass: 2,25 kg
Gestation: 30 days

Squirrels

Of the six squirrel species found in southern Africa I have dealt with only two, the ground squirrel *(Xerus inauris)* and the tree squirrel *(Paraxerus cepapi)*. The others are the Kaokoveld ground squirrel *(Xerus princeps)*, the red bush squirrel *(Paraxerus palliatus)*, Kuhl's tree squirrel *(Funisciurus congicus)* (from northern Namibia and further north), and the red-legged sun squirrel *(Heliosciurus rufobrachium)* from Mocambique and south-eastern Zimbabwe.

Ground Squirrel
Waaierstertgrondeekhoring
(Xerus inauris)

Diet:
Vegetarian; roots, bulbs.

General:
These squirrels are purely terrestrial and live in open, dry habitat, from the northern Cape, south-western Botswana and Namibia.
Highly sociable, they live in large groups in burrows up to 183 m in length, which they excavate themselves.
Strictly diurnal, they are wary although casual about concealing themselves.

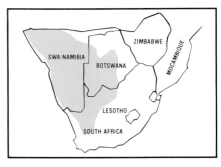

Description:
Length: 20 to 29 cm
Mass: 1 kg

Faeces:
1,5 cm long, 0,5 cm wide.

Tree Squirrel
Boomeekhoring
(Paraxerus cepapi)

Shona: Tsindi   **Ndebele:** Ubusinti   **Venda:** Tshithura
Shangaan: Sindyane
Lozi: Kamale   **Yei:** Unshindi

Diet:
Vegetarian; leaves, wild fruits, roots.

General:
Solitary or in pairs. Diurnal. Arboreal.
Spend a large amount of time on the ground in search of food.
When disturbed make great haste in retreating to the nearest tree.
Live in holes in trees, lining the nest with grasses. Have a peculiar call which is often mistaken for that of a bird.
They are preyed upon by the black mamba, hawks, genets, wild cats, pythons and mongooses. Its distribution extends from northern Zululand, Mocambique, eastern Transvaal, Rustenburg and Waterberg districts, through to south-eastern Botswana and Zimbabwe.

 Fore

Actual Size

Hind

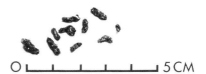

O ⊢——⊣——⊣——⊣——⊣——⊣ 5 CM

R.S.

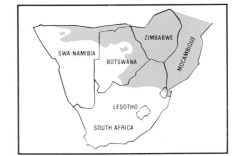

Description:
Overall length: 35 cm
Mass: 0,2 kg

Nothing is wasted in the bush; even if the waiting is long.

◄ Young scholars explore the wilderness. Photo: D. Richards.

Leopard kill. Small spotted Genet.

Springhaas
(Pedetes capensis)

Ndebele: Umahelane   **Shona:** Nhire, Gwidzu
Zulu: Ndlulane   **Shangaan:** Xindjengwe
Southern Sotho: Tshipjane   **Tswana:** Tshipô
Venda: Khadzimutavha   **Siswati:** Ndlulwane
Lozi: Sinkuyu   **Yei:** Unkuyu

Diet:
Vegetarian; mainly the stems of grasses, bulbs and roots.

General:
Purely nocturnal. Living in pairs, often in large communities, in burrows which they excavate in sandy soils. Swift kangaroo-like creatures with acute senses. Their flesh is much sought after by certain tribes and in Botswana it provides a considerable part of the Bushman's diet.

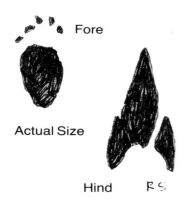

Fore

Actual Size

Hind   R ℅

0 |___|___|___|___|___| 5 CM

Description:
Overall length: 70 cm
Mass: 3 kg
Gestation: 45 days.

Spoor:
Three-toed impression, hind foot.

Faeces:
2 cm long.

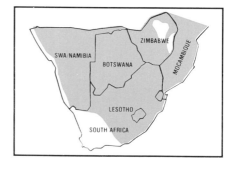

36

Greater Canerat
Grootrietrot

(Thryonomys swinderianus)

Shona: Tsenzi **Ndebele:** Ivondo **Zulu, Siswati:** Vondo
Shangaan: Nhleti **Tswana:** Bodi **Venda:** Tshedzi
Transvaal Sotho: Tswidi
Lozi: Siumbi¹ **Yei:** Unsenze

Diet:
Reeds, aquatic grasses, fruits, bark, other types of grass, and crops.
They are well known for crop raiding, particularly sugar cane.

General:
Mainly nocturnal. Gregarious but often found singly.
Swim exceptionally well and will take to water readily. Their presence is noticeable by the 'runs' they create through grass and general vegetation.
Mainly found on the edges of swamps, vleis, river banks and dams.
The young, up to four at birth, are born in burrows lined with grasses.
Widespread throughout southern Africa.
Preyed upon by a large range of carnivores, principally eagles and pythons.
Highly prized by certain tribes as a food source.

O |___|___|___|___|___| 5 CM

Description:
Overall length: 60 cm
Mass: 4 to 5 kg
Gestation: 90 days

Spoor:
Four-toed impression, 5 cm long.

Faeces:
Similar to the springhare 2 cm long.

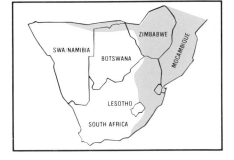

37

Dassies in their rocky home.

Baboons possess larger canines than those of a lion.

Hippopotamus; Nature's natural dredgers. Photo: P. Dutton.

Fore

Actual Size

Hind

0 |___|___|___|___|___| 5 CM

40

Porcupine
Ystervark
(Hystrix africaeaustralis)

Zulu: Nungu   **Siswati:** Ngungubane   **Shangaan:** Nungu
Tswana; Transvaal Sotho: Noko   **Venda:** Nungu
Lozi: Sinuku   **Yei:** Unungu

Diet:
Vegetarian. Capable of doing great damage to crops. Fond of bark of trees. Will gnaw bones and ivory which accounts for the absence of these when finding a dead elephant in a remote area.

General:
The porcupine is the largest African rodent, which has successfully adapted and has a wide habitat tolerance. It is distributed throughout southern Africa.
Armed with lethal quills which it rattles when annoyed or alarmed. If this fails it will attack in a sideways and backwards action, in an attempt to impale their attacker. It does not shoot its quills. Its principal enemies are the lion and the leopard, although they attack at their own peril.
The porcupine frequents disused antbear holes, holes which it has dug itself, caves or rocky crevices. Here it raises its young or lies up.
Found alone, in pairs or in small groups.
The porcupine is nocturnal.

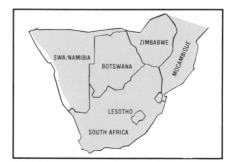

Wood and bone gnawed by porcupine.

Description:
Overall length: 80 cm
Mass: Up to 18 kg
Gestation: 93 to 94 days
(R. van Aarde, pers. comm.)

Spoor:
Hind foot elongated, up to 9 cm long; forefoot 5 to 6 cm long.
Faeces:
Easily recognisable, being shaped like a series of fibrous, elongated fire crackers, often attached.

Blue wildebeest killed by lions.

◄ Sunset over the Shashe River, Tuli Block, Botswana

Blond Kalahari lion.

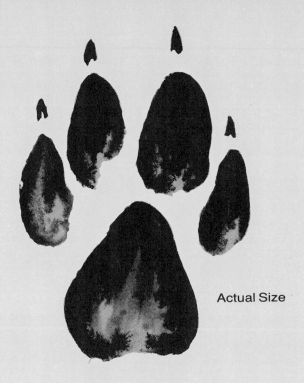

Actual Size

Wild Dog
Wildehond
(Lycaon pictus)

Shona: Mhumhi **Ndebele:** Inganyana **Shangaan:** Hlolwa
Tswana: Letharelwa **Venda:** Dalerwa **Zulu:** Nkontshane
Sotho: Klalerwa **Siswati:** Budzatje
Lozi: Liakanyani **Yei:** Umenzi

Diet:
They prey on a wide range from small to large mammals and domestic stock. They will also consume the prey of other predators. Parents regurgitate food for the litter.

General:
Killers in carnival suits, wild dogs have a poor reputation and have been reduced to very low numbers in South Africa. Game farms have also eliminated them which is most short-sighted as they move around continuously. They are fearless and have considerable stamina which is required for running down their prey. They have a well-ordered social structure and may be found in packs of up to 30 to 40 individuals. Their inquisitive nature may cause alarm, but no case exists where humans have come to harm. They make a soft clicking sound and have a deep, hoarse bark. Good eyesight. This rare species' range has been very much reduced and it probably occurs only in reasonable numbers in Botswana.

Description:
Shoulder height: 65 cm
Mass: 24 to 30 kg
Gestation: About 60 days

Spoor:
Neat, elongated track with distinctive claw marks.

Faeces:
Dog-like, elongated and often full of hair.

• Endangered species.

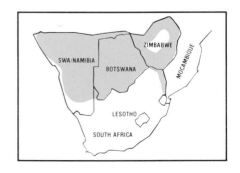

Burchell's zebra.

◀ Rhino rubbing post.

Female Steenbok.

Cape Fox
Silwervos
(Vulpes chama)

Southern Sotho: Mophèmè

Diet:
Small mammals, insects, birds, eggs of ground birds.
General:

The only true fox to be found in southern Africa inhabiting dry, open veld and the Kalahari savanna, northern Cape, Orange Free State, southern Botswana and South West Africa. They are mainly nocturnal and are found singly or in pairs. They live and raise their young in burrows, but will also lie up under dense scrub. Their voice is not unlike that of the European fox.

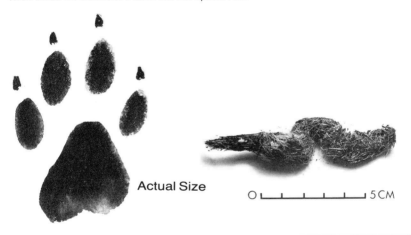

Actual Size

O └──┴──┴──┴──┘ 5 CM

Description:
Shoulder height: 30 to 33 cm
Mass: 3,6 to 4,5 kg
Gestation: About 56 days — 3 to 5 young in a litter.

Spoor:
They have 5 toes on the forefeet and 4 on the hind. Similar to that of the black-backed jackal but slightly narrower.

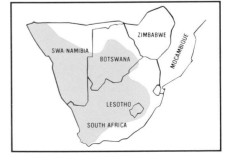

Springbok.

raffe with redbilled oxpeckers, often found in the company of Giraffe.

Spotted hyaena: regurgitated hair and bone.

Actual Size

O |___|___|___|___|___|___|___| 5 CM

Bat-eared Fox
Bakoorvos
(Otocyon megalotis)

Transvaal Sotho: Motlhose **Tswana:** Tlhose **Ndebele:** Unga
Shona: Gava

Diet:
Eats insects, small rodents, fruits, ground-nesting birds, small reptiles and larvae. Their large, well-developed ears enable them to detect underground prey which they then dig out.

General:
They have the ability to twist and turn whilst running after prey or when escaping any predator. The bushy, black-tipped tail, black-edged ears and blackish legs make this animal easily distinguishable. They are mainly nocturnal and occur in pairs or small groups. They live in burrows which they dig themselves, in old antbear holes or under bushes. Their call is not a howl, but a series of soft, shrill who-who sounds. They are to be found in Botswana, South West Africa, northern and south western Cape, the western fringe of Zimbabwe, Transvaal (mainly in the west) and the Orange Free State. They are heavily trapped in Botswana for their attractive pelts which are made into karosses. Their senses are well-developed. The bat-eared fox is not, as its name implies, a true fox.

Dung heap of bat-eared fox showing undigested exoskeleton of myriopoda.

Description:
Shoulder height: 30 cm
Mass: 4 kg
Gestation: 60 to 70 days

Spoor:
Neat, narrow foot.

Civet dung. The civet will utilize the same spot daily.

Cheetah (Acinonyx jubatus). An endangered species.

Baboon at sunset.

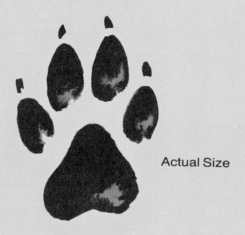

Actual Size

O⊢——⊢——⊢——⊢——⊢——⊣5 CM

Black-backed Jackal
Rooijakkals
(Canis mesomelas)

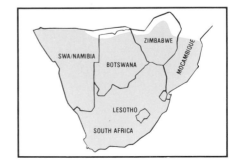

Zulu: Mpungutshe, Khanka **Siswati:** Mpungutje **Shangaan:** Impungutshe
Ndebele: Ikhanka **Shona:** Hungubwe **Tswana:** Phokojwe
Venda: Phungubwe **Sotho:** Phokobje, Phokojoe

Diet:
Carrion, rodents, reptiles, game-birds, insects, eggs, fruit, hares. They hunt
young antelope and will prey on small, young livestock.

General:
A handsome, widely-distributed species which occurs throughout southern
Africa. Their distinctive cry is well known and they communicate with an
elaborate vocabulary. They are mainly nocturnal and are found singly or in pairs.
Large numbers will congregate at a carcass. They are cunning and swift and will
wait in the wings for lions to finish eating, often darting in to snatch a morsel.
They lie up during the day under low bushes. Their young are born in abandoned
antbear holes. They drink water regularly. Their sight, scent and hearing are
acute.

Description:
Shoulder height: 40 cm
Mass: Up to 11 kg
Gestation: 60 days with up to 6
pups in a litter.

Spoor:
Neat, small, dog-like tracks 5 cm
long.

Faeces:
Small dog-like in appearance.

Desert elephants of the Kaokoveld. Photo: F.C. Eloff.

◀ Rhino rubbing post.

Leopard; the silent killer.

Actual Size

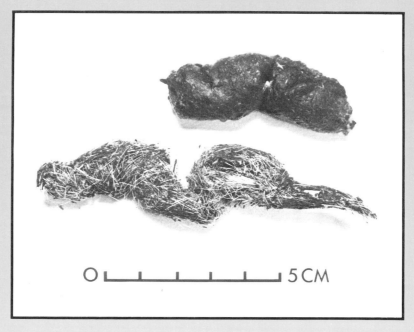

O ⊢—⊢—⊢—⊢—⊢—⊢ 5CM

Side-striped Jackal
Witkwasjakkals
(Canis adustus)

Zulu: Mpungutshe **Venda:** Dabe **Tswana:** Rantalàje
Shangaan: Hlati **Shona:** Gava
Ndebele: Ikhanka **Siswati:** Inkalwane
Lozi: Luwawa

Diet:
Scavengers, but their diet will also include reptiles, rodents, insects and wild fruits. They are dependent on water. They do not prey on domestic stock as the black-backed jackal does.

General:
Fairly silent animals, they lack the customary howl of the black-backed jackal. They are found singly or in pairs. The Bayei people of the Okavango Swamps believe their appearance signals the presence of lion. They are lighter in mass and do not have the distinctive saddle of the black-backed jackal. Being nocturnal, they rest during the day in antbear holes or in thickets and are not often seen. Has a distinctive white tip to the tail.

Description:
Shoulder height: 40 cm
Mass: 8 kg
Gestation: 60 days

Spoor:
Identical to that of the black-backed jackal.
Approximately 5 cm long.

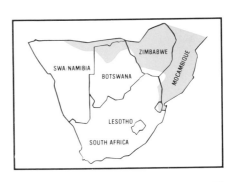

61

Bat-eared fox.

◀ Young Kudu bull.

Spotted hyaena dung.

Striped Polecat
Stinkmuishond
(Ictonyx striatus)

Also called: Zorilla, Cape Polecat, African Skunk.
Zulu: Qaqa, Ngankakazana **Shona:** Ehidembo **Ndebele:** Iqaqa
Tswana: Nakedi **Venda:** Thuri **Transvaal Sotho:** Nakedi **Siswati:** Licaca
Lozi: Kangamba

Diet:
Rodents, reptiles, insects, birds, frogs. Fond of poultry and adept at killing snakes.

General:
Nocturnal, rests during the day in holes in the ground, in rocky crevices and in dense bush. A handsome animal with black and white vertical markings with a well-bushed tail. Capable of shamming death and, when angered or cornered, retaliates by ejecting a powerful, vile scent from anal glands. Anything getting in the way, will carry the smell for days. Its voice is a high-pitched scream. A useful creature — best left alone. Found singly or in pairs. Widespread distribution.

Actual Size

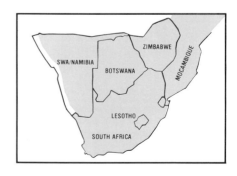

O └─┴─┴─┴─┴─┘ 5 CM

Description:
Length: 70 cm (overall)
Shoulder height: 10 cm
Mass: 1,3 kg

Spoor:
3 cm long, claws well defined.

Striped Weasel
Slangmuishond
(Poecilogale albinucha)

Also called: Snake weasel

Zulu: Nyengelezi

Diet:
Rodents, reptiles.

General:
Slender and lighter than the striped polecat, it also ejects an evil-smelling fluid. Little is known about this species which is mainly nocturnal. They occur singly or in pairs and excavate their own burrows. Distribution is widespread.

Actual Size

Description:
Overall length: 50 cm
Shoulder height: 7 cm
Mass: 0,3 kg
Gestation: 33 to 37 days

Spoor:
Narrower than that of the polecat and about 1 cm shorter. Claws not as well defined.

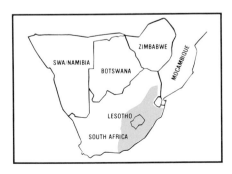

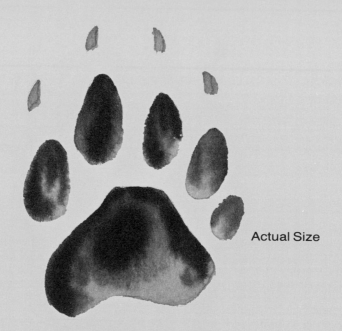

Actual Size

O   5CM

Honey Badger
Ratel
(Mellivora capensis)

Shona: Sere, Tsere **Ndebele:** Ulinda **Zulu, Siswati:** Nsele
Tswana: Matswani, Matshwane **Venda:** Tshiselele
Shangaan: Shidzidzi **Transvaal Sotho:** Magôgê
Lozi: Sikape **Yei:** Umbuli

Diet:
A wide variety of food constitutes the diet of this active animal, such as reptiles, insects, larvae of dung beetles, eggs, ground birds, wild fruit, scorpions, grubs and the honey of bees. They have an interesting relationship with the honey-guide which they follow in search of the hive. Fond of poultry.

General:
The distribution is widespread in Africa. Honey badgers are fearless, display considerable aggression and have a powerful bite. Their loose skin enables them to turn easily upon anything that attempts to take hold of them. They will also turn and attack humans and vehicles. They are best left alone. Honey badgers are good at digging and, like the mongoose, are fond of digging out the hardened dung beetle balls in search of larvae. They live in holes where, usually, they lie up during the day being mainly nocturnal. Their sense of smell is acute.

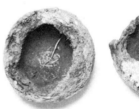

Dung beetle balls

Description:
Length: 80 cm
Shoulder height: 26 cm
Mass: 9 kg
Gestation: About 180 days

Spoor:
8 cm long. Hind foot longer. Fore foot long and broad.

Faeces
Collected in the Okavango.

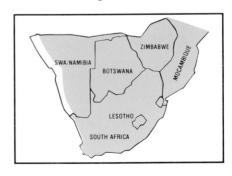

Actual Size

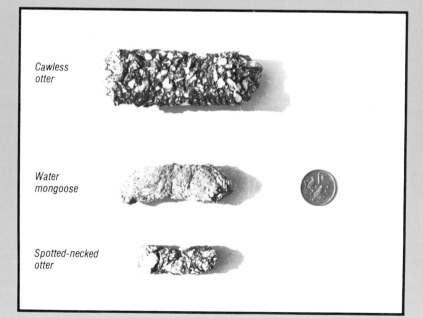

Cawless
otter

Water
mongoose

Spotted-necked
otter

Spotted-necked Otter
Kleinotter
(Lutra maculicollis)

Siswati: Ntsini   **Zulu:** Ntini
Lozi: Nibi   **Yei:** Ungwanda

Diet:
Crabs, fish, frogs and aquatic insects.

General:
A nocturnal species found singly or in small groups. They inhabit swamps, streams, backwaters of perennial rivers and lakes and create channels through the vegetation leading to the water's edge. This species is more aquatic by nature than the clawless otter. They are distributed from the eastern Cape to Natal and Swaziland.

Description:
Overall length: 96 cm
Mass: 9 kg
Gestation: Unknown

Spoor:
They have webbed toes armed with sharp, short claws.

Faeces:
Collected by D. Rowe-Rowe.

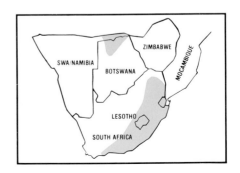

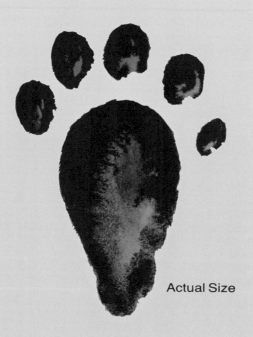

Actual Size

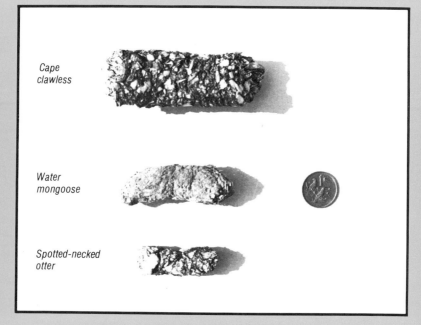

Cape
clawless

Water
mongoose

Spotted-necked
otter

Cape Clawless Otter
Groototter
(Aonyx capensis)

Shona: Mbiti   **Ndebele:** Intini   **Zulu:** Ntini
Siswati: Ntsini   **Venda:** Nivho   **Tswana:** Nyedi
Lozi: Mbao   **Yei:** Utungwa

Diet:
Crabs, molluscs, fish, aquatic birds, rodents and frogs.

General:
Cape clawless otters are both nocturnal and diurnal. They do not confine themselves to water and wander some distance inland in search of food. They are
excellent swimmers and their resting places are to be found amongst thick
vegetation alongside the water, in hollows of tree roots and crevices. They do
not excavate burrows. These are robust animals with well-developed canines
and an acute sense of smell and hearing. They are widely distributed throughout Africa in areas of permanent water

Cape clawless otter habitat. Quiet backwaters.

Description:
Overall length: 1,2 m
Mass: 18 kg
Gestation: 60 days

Spoor:
The hind feet are partially
webbed and the forefeet
clawless, 7 to 8 cm long.

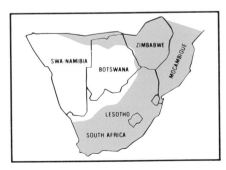

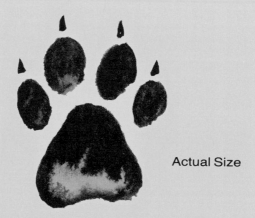

Actual Size

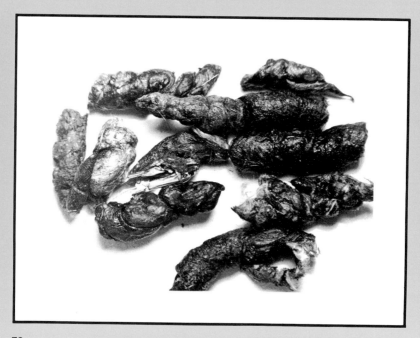

African Civet
Siwetkat
(Civettictis civetta)

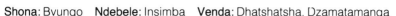

Shona: Bvungo   **Ndebele:** Insimba   **Venda:** Dhatshatsha, Dzamatamanga
Northern Sotho: Tsaparangaka
Siswati: Lifungwe   **Shangaan:** Fungwe
Lozi: Nyangongo

Diet:
Mainly carnivorous. Snakes, rodents, birds, insects, chongololos, sun spiders, small mammals, fruits, other vegetable matter and berries. Fond of raiding poultry and bush kitchens. As with genets one is well advised to lock away foodstuffs. They wander over great distances when feeding.

General:
Civets are widespread in their distribution and common. They are attractive animals with bushy coats, spotted on the body with stripes on the legs and tail which is bushy. Secretive, nocturnal. Civets lie up during the day in tall grass, bush reed beds and holes in the ground. Good swimmers. Cry is a low growl or a loud cough. Secretes an oily tar-like substance from peri-anal glands when excited.

Description:
Shoulder height: 38 cm
Mass: 15 kg
Gestation: Unknown. Up to 4 at birth. August to October.

Spoor:
4 cm long, circular track with nails evident.

Faeces:
Large for such an animal.
Defecate in middens.
Often on high vantage points,
easily recognised by the
presence of millipedes
exoskeletons.

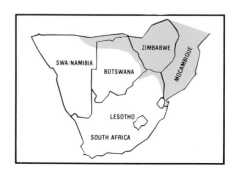

Genetta tigrina

Genetta genetta

Large-spotted Genet
Grootkolmuskeljaatkat
(Genetta tigrina)

Other name: Rusty-spotted genet
Siswati: Insimba   **Lozi:** Sipa
Yei: Unsiimba

Small-spotted Genet
Kleinkolmuskeljaatkat
(Genetta genetta)

Actual Size

Shona: Tsimba   **Ndebele:** Insimba   **Tswana:** Tsipa
Shangaan: Nsimba   **Sotho:** Tshipa   **Venda:** Tsimba
Lozi: Sipa   **Yei:** Unsiimba

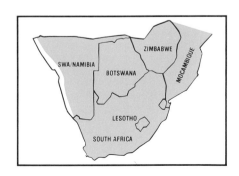

Diet:
Rodents, reptiles, insects, birds, frogs and wild fruits. Fond of poultry and will raid camp kitchens.

General:
Widely distributed, nocturnal and equally at home on the ground or climbing trees. Mainly solitary. They are bold and skilled poultry thieves. The large-spotted genet has a black-tipped tail whilst that of the small-spotted genet is white. The large-spotted genet is rusty coloured.

Description:
Length: 90 cm
Mass: 2 kg
Gestation: Unknown

Spoor:
Similar for both species, 3 cm long.

75

Actual Size

Suricate
Stokstertmeerkat

(Suricata suricatta)

Southern Sotho: Toli   **Transvaal Sotho:** Letoto
Tswana: Sie

Diet:
Insects, small birds and to a lesser extent, small mammals, the eggs of ground birds and reptiles.

General:
Highly sociable, living in large colonies. They will excavate their own burrows and will also utilize the burrows of the ground squirrel *(Xerus inauris).*
Suricates are entirely diurnal and their natural enemies are the large raptors.
Fond of sitting on their haunches and chattering — often stand fully upright.
A small, compact animal with dark bands across the back, eye patches and short tail with a black tip.

Burrow in the Kalahari.

Description:
Length: 45 cm
Mass: 0,62 to 0,97 kg
Gestation: About 84 days.

Spoor:
Compact, neat with conspicuous claws.

Faeces:
Compact, small droppings comprising a variety of matter.

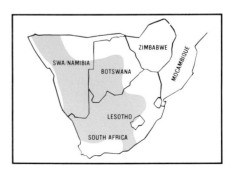

Meller's Mongoose
Meller se Muishond
(Rhynchogale melleri)

80 cm

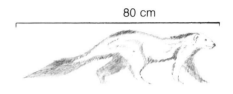

Diet:
Termites, small vertebrates.

General:
Found in the Transvaal, Mocambique and Zimbabwe.
Frequents forested savanna. A fairly large mongoose with a long bushy tail with coarse body hair. Solitary, nocturnal creatures occasionally diurnal. Little is known about this mongoose.

O └─┴─┴─┴─┴─┘ 5 CM

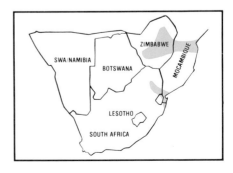

Description:
Length: 80 cm
Mass: 2,7 kg

Yellow Mongoose
Rooimeerkat
(Cynictis penicillata)

Tswana: Motodi   Transvaal Sotho: Pipi
Other names: Bushy-tailed mongoose, Geelmuishond

50 – 65 cm

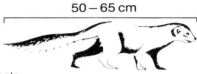

Diet:
Termites, other insects, frogs, birds, rodents.

General:
Generally diurnal. Lives in colonies in open country from the Cape, Orange Free State, Transvaal into South West Africa. Absent in Natal. Fond of burrowing. Yellowish-brown long coat with fairly large ears. Figures are not available on mass, but it is a small mongoose with a short pointed muzzle. Short tail, white-tipped. Endemic to southern Africa.

O |⎯⎯|⎯⎯|⎯⎯|⎯⎯| 5 CM

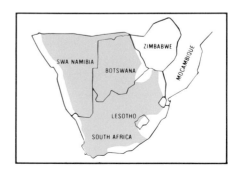

Description:
Length: 50 – 65 cm

Spoor:
Four toes on hind foot.

Faeces:
Dung is deposited in various areas.

Selous' Mongoose
Kleinwitstertmuishond
(Paracynictis selousi)

Shona: Jerenyenje   **Zulu:** Nsengane   **Ndebele:** Duhwa, I(bu) Chakide

Diet:
Insects, larvae, small rodents, birds.

General:
Nocturnal. Found singly or in pairs. Selous' mongoose has long, curved claws adapted for digging. Unlike other mongooses, they dig tunnels which interlink to form burrows. They are widespread in Zimbabwe although uncommon elsewhere. Found in the Transvaal, Botswana, South West Africa and Angola.

O |___|___|___|___|___| 5 CM

Actual Size

Description:
Length: 70 cm overall.
Shoulder height: 20 cm.
Mass: Up to 2,7 kg.

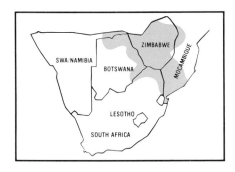

Spoor:
Distinctive curved claws, four toes to each foot.

Small Grey Mongoose
Kaapse Grysmuishond
(Galerella pulverulenta)

50-65 cm

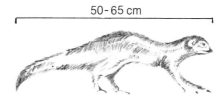

Diet:
Rodents, snakes, lizards, hares, insects.

General:
Diurnal, terrestrial, found singly, in pairs or in small family groups. They are shy and elusive and are more stockily built than the slender mongoose. The general colour is mottled grey – the hairs ringed black and white. They inhabit savanna in the southern half of the Cape Province.

O └─┴─┴─┴─┴─┘ 5 CM

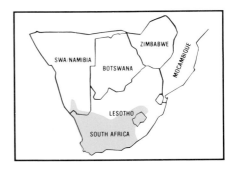

Description:
Length: 35 cm (without tail).

Water Mongoose
Kommetjiegat-
muishond

70 cm

(Atilax paludinosus)

Shona: Chidzvororo   **Ndebele:** Imvuzi   **Xhosa:** Vuzi
Zulu: Mvuzi   **Tswana:** Tshagane   **Sotho:** Motswitswi
Siswati: Liduha   **Lozi:** Mukala   **Yei:** Ugwagara

Diet:
Crabs, fish, reptiles, insects, rodents, birds and wild fruit. They prey on the eggs of the crocodile.

General:
They are solitary, adept at digging and are good swimmers with well-developed cheek teeth for crushing crabs and beetles. They emit a strong scent from an anal gland when disturbed. This gland is also used to mark territories. They have a short tapering tail with a robust, dark brown body.

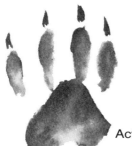

Actual size

0 └─┴─┴─┴─┴─┘ 5 CM

Description:
Length: 70 cm
Shoulder height: 15 cm
Mass: 2,5 kg

Spoor:
Pointed toes, which are well adapted to searching for prey under water, 3 cm long.

Faeces:
Noticeable from the remains of shell. All mongoose faeces invariably have a strong odour.

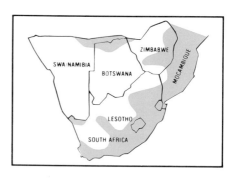

White-tailed Mongoose
Witstertmuishond
(Ichneumia albicauda)

Xhosa: Ngqwalashu **Zulu:** Gqalashu **Ndebele:** Ubachakide
Shona: Jerenyenje **Tswana:** Tshagane **Venda:** Mutsherere
Shangaan: Tlolota **Siswati:** Liduha

1,2 m

Diet:
Poultry raiders, frogs, crabs, rodents, birds, insects, fish and reptiles, berries and fruits. They are also poultry raiders.

General:
Mainly nocturnal and solitary. Frequent rivers, marshes, vleis and well-bushed areas. They wander fair distances from water in search of food. They rest during the day in holes and cavities. They are darkish grey in colour with darker underparts and a white tip to the tail.

Actual size

O ∟ ⅃ ⅃ ⅃ ⅃ ⅃ 5 CM

Description:
Length: 1,2 m
Shoulder height: 25 cm
Mass: 4 kg

Spoor:
Five toes to fore and hind feet.
Long curved claws the tips of
which are conspicuous, 4 cm
long.

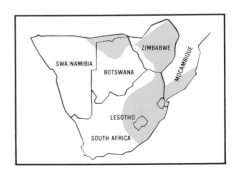

Large Grey Mongoose
Grootgrysmuishond
(Herpestes ichneumon)

Zulu: Nhlangala   **Tswana:** Tshagane

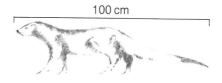

100 cm

Diet:
Fish, crabs, birds, rodents, reptiles, insects. Usually frequents water.

General:
A diurnal species found singly or in pairs. They swim well and favour riverine vegetation, reed beds. They are entirely terrestrial and have a widespread distribution. They are grey in colour with a black tip to the tail and blackish face and feet.

Actual Size

0 ⌐__I__I__I__I__⌐ 5 CM

Description:
Length: 1 m
Mass: 3 kg

Spoor:
Elongated with pointed claws,
spoor 4 cm long.

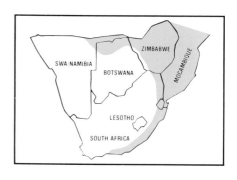

Slender Mongoose
Rooimuishond
(Galerella sanguineus)

Zulu: Chakide   **Siswati:** Chakidze   **Venda:** Khohe   **Shona:** Hovo
Ndebele: Iwobo   **Tswana:** Kganwe   **Sotho:** Kgano   **Shangaan:** Mangovo
Other names: Black-tipped mongoose.

Diet:
Snakes, rodents, insects, scorpions. An aggressive hunter capable of dispatching mamba and other dangerous snakes. Prone to attack from raptors. A notorious thief of young poultry.

General:
This is a diurnal, solitary species which has a wide habitat tolerance, and which is not greatly dependent on water. Terrestrial, they will take to trees when in search of birds' eggs. Like most mongooses they are prone to rabies. They have a distinctive black tip to the tail. Another form *Galerella sanguineus nigrata* from the Kaokoveld, is dark, with a broad black line on the back and with a black-tipped tail.

Actual Size

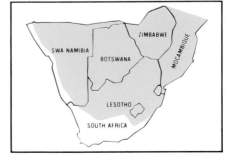

O └─┴─┴─┴─┴─┘ 5 CM

Description:
Length: 60 cm (including tail)
Shoulder height: 13 cm
Mass: 5 kg
Gestation: about 45 days

Spoor:
Forefeet claws, sharp and curved. Neat, narrow track, 3 cm long.

85

Banded Mongoose
Gebande Muishond
(Mungos mungo)

Ndebele: Usikibhoror **Shona:** Dzvoro **Tswana:** Totohto
Venda: Tshihoho **Shangaan:** Nkala **Zulu:** Buhala
Lozi: Kaâalañati

Diet:
Primarily an insect eater, the larvae of beetles form a favourite part of their diet. Dung beetle balls are a prime target. They also eat rodents, snails, roots, wild fruit, reptiles, scorpions, and birds' eggs which they break open by rolling them through their hind legs against rocks. They are noisy when feeding.

General:
They are inquisitive, gregarious and are found in groups of upwards to forty. They live in antbear holes, termite holes or holes they dig themselves. They are attacked by predator birds and, in turn, will defend themselves vigorously. They frequently stand on their hind legs to obtain a better view. These diurnal, smallish mongooses have distinctive bands from the shoulders to the base of the tail. All senses are good and like most mongooses, they are adept at killing snakes.

Actual Size

O⌐_i___i___i___i___i___i⌐ 5 CM

Description:
Length: 60 cm
Shoulder height: 13 cm
Mass: 2 kg
Gestation: About 60 days

Spoor:
Foreclaws twice as long as the hind claws, 3 cm long.

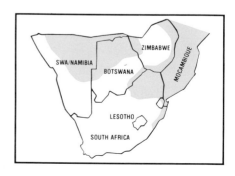

Dwarf Mongoose
Dwergmuishond
(Helogale parvula)

Sotho: Motswitswane   **Ndebele:** Iduha   **Venda:** Matswi

Diet:
Insects, grubs, rodents, wild fruit, eggs — they eat virtually anything they find. Independent of water.

General:
The smallest of the African mongooses, they are found in large family groups and use antbear holes as homes. They are diurnal, bold and tireless in their search for food. Their body colour is a uniform brown to reddish brown. Like other mongooses, they utter growls and sit up on their hind legs when disturbed.

Actual Size

O └──┴──┴──┴──┴──┘ 5 CM

Description:
Length: 40 cm
Shoulder height: 7 cm
Mass: 0,3 kg
Gestation: 45 to 50 days

Spoor:
Small track, long and sharp claws, soles of feet naked to the heel, spoor 2 cm long.

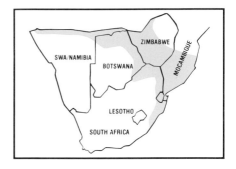

Actual Size

O ⌞_____⌟ 5 CM

Aardwolf
(Proteles cristatus)

Shona: Mwena **Ndebele:** Inthuhu **Venda:** Tshivingwi
Xhosa, Zulu: Nehi **Siswati:** Ngci **Tswana:** Thuku
Lozi: Mutosi **Yei:** Unshushi

Diet:
Termites.

General:
Aardwolves have fairly long canine teeth which are weak and there is no evidence available to suggest that they prey on livestock. The teeth are so poorly developed that it is most doubtful whether they could even cope with carrion. Timid and inoffensive, these animals occur singly or in pairs. They are nocturnal and during the day lie up in burrows which they excavate, or in disused antbear holes. If disturbed and excited, they emit a strong odour from anal glands. This is not as strong, however, as that of the striped polecat. Their habitat includes desert, plains and thornveld. Their voice is a bark like a dog, but they are also capable of roaring. The anal gland is used to mark their territory, the pasting usually done on a grass stalk. (see photograph)

Description:
Shoulder height: 50 cm
Mass: up to 11 kg
Gestation: 60 days

Spoor:
The aardwolf has a spoor not unlike that of a hyaena but less than half the length. Four toes on the forelegs and five on the hind legs.

Aardwolf pasting on grass stalks.

Faeces:
They cover their faeces with sand and a large proportion of the scat is pure sand which is taken in whilst licking up termites.

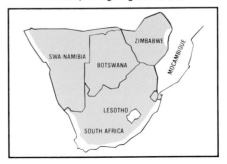

89

Spoor 11 cm long

Spotted Hyaena
Gevlekte Hiëna
(Crocuta crocuta)

Xhosa, Zulu, Siswati; Sindebele: Mpisi   **Shangaan:** Mhisi
Sotho, Tswana: Phiri   **Shona:** Bere   **Venda:** Phele
Lozi: Sitongwani   **Yei:** Umpuru

Diet:
Carnivorous — predator and scavenger. Will eat large amounts of bone with no difficulty.

General: *See over*

Description:
Shoulder height: 70 to 81 cm
Mass: 65 to 70 kg
Gestation: 105 days, 2 to 3 young.

Spoor:
Much like a large dog, broad in the fore main pad. Claw tips showing distinctly, identical to the brown hyaena but larger. Hind foot distinctly smaller than forefoot.

Faeces:
Green in colour when fresh, it turns pure white with age because of the mineral and bone content. Conspicuous latrine areas are usually found in open areas, and they urinate at regular places. Whole faeces of hair are common and vomit consisting of hair, bone fragments and hooves is occasionally found.

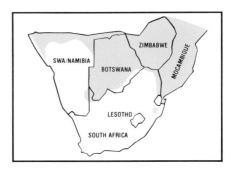

General:

Found throughout the African savanna. They are noisy animals with a variety of calls, moans, laughs and shrieks. They both scavenge and hunt, feeding on anything they find. They have powerful jaws which are capable of cracking the leg bones of giraffe. They are primarily nocturnal creatures, emerging from antbear holes, caves and rocky areas at nightfall. Where they are unmolested, they can be seen during daylight hours. They possess excellent sight, hearing and sense of smell. Although they are cunning, powerful and treacherous, they fear lions and wild dogs. When camped out in the open at night, caution must be exercised and foodstuffs, meat, etc., should not be left lying about. If sleeping 'under the stars', it is advisable to keep a good fire going and to mount night watches. They can become extremely bold when hungry and there have been cases of sleeping people losing part of their face. They are swift animals capable of a speed of up to 45 km/h. They are found singly, in pairs and in groups up to 30 at a kill. They are observant and watch vultures descending on to a kill; they also follow lions calling. Hyaenas kill a higher percentage of their prey than they actually scavenge. They have distinct territories, but clan structures overlap with varying degrees of tolerance. The females are larger than the males and dominate. Spotted hyaenas are not dependent on water but will drink regularly when it is available. The undertakers of the African savanna, these interesting animals deserve a better understanding and much more is yet to be learnt about them.

The spotted hyaenas have extremely powerful jaws and tins present no problems to these foraging animals.

Spotted hyaenas occupy abandoned antbear holes where they set up homes.

Bone fragments found in spotted hyaena faeces.

Actual Size

Brown Hyaena
Strandjut
(Hyaena brunnea)

Ndebele: Impisi   Shona: Bere   Sotho: Phirbjokwane
Tswana: Tlonkana   Bushman: Nutsa

Diet:
Wide variety of food — insects, birds, eggs, wild fruits, springhares, domestic stock, antelope, carrion (scavenged vertebrate remains). Along the coast of Namibia and the Cape, it feeds on the washed up remains of marine animals from where it acquired the name 'strandjut'.

General:
Recent studies have revealed the species to be more abundant than previously believed. It is a shy, nocturnal animal which lives up in antbear holes by day. It is well adapted to the dry regions of southern Africa and areas devoid of surface water. As in the spotted hyaena, it has a well-developed digestive system, with an efficient olfactory system for locating carrion. It is found in Zimbabwe, Angola, Botswana, Namibia, the Transvaal and northern Cape across to the Atlantic. Far more silent than the spotted hyaena, it utters resonant whoofs. The distinctive 'laugh' of the spotted hyaena is absent.

Description:
Shoulder height: 71 to 81 cm
Mass: 50 to 56 kg
Gestation: 90 days, 2 to 3 young.

Spoor:
Dog-like with short, blunt non-retractile claws.

Faeces:
Green when fresh, turning white. Paste secretions on grass stalks and defecate at latrine areas.

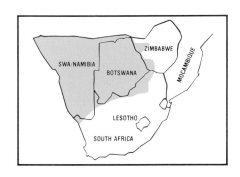

Spoor 12 cm long

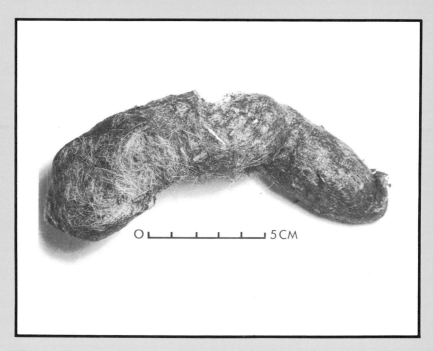

0   5 CM

Lion
Leeu
(Panthera leo)

Shona: Shumba **Ndebele:** Isilwane **Zulu:** Ngonyama
Siswati: Ngwenyama **Shangaan:** Nghala, N'shumba **Sotho:** Tau
Venda: Ndau **Tswana:** Tau **Lozi:** Tau **Yei:** Undavu

Diet:
Lions are not fussy and will eat virtually anything including carrion when hungry, although they usually prey on medium-sized to large-hoofed animals. In the Okavango they pull down lone buffalo bulls and bulls on the outskirts of herds. Giraffe also fall prey to lion although the lion is mindful of their savage kick. Hans Bufè *(pers. comm.)* observed lion feeding on a crocodile on the banks of the Luangwa river. They hunt, in the main, at night. Lions drink regularly when water is available, though they are capable of going without water for long periods in deserts and arid areas. Prof. Fritz Eloff *(pers. comm.)* has observed the Kalahari lions eating tsamma melons and gemsbok cucumbers.

Description:
Shoulder height: 91 to 100 cm
Mass: males 181 to 227 kg
females 113 to 136 kg
Gestation: 100 – 119 days.
Breed throughout the year.

Spoor:
Unmistakable large pug marks and in spite of their size, they tread lightly. Claws are fully sheathed.

Faeces:
Similar to that of the leopard, but larger. When lions have consumed a fair amount of blood, the dung is usually very black and strong-smelling. The dung also turns white when there is a high calcium content. Pieces of whole hair are passed without other matter being present. Faeces sometimes consist of 'bundles' of porcupine quills.

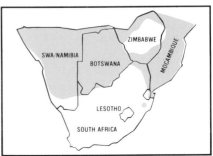

General

Lions are both diurnal and nocturnal. They are highly social and are found in small prides and groups of up to twenty individuals. They prey on a wide range of species including small rodents. They have excellent sight, sense of smell and hearing. One can, however, stumble on sleeping lions or when one is heading into a stiff wind.

So much has been written about lions that one risks repetition, however, for the benefit of those who might encounter lions on foot, the following significant observations should be noted.

Should you come suddenly on lions, you should remain absolutely still — under **NO** circumstances run. Should you be with a party, everyone should be so instructed before you set off.

Should you come across a lioness with cubs, she may charge. I have experienced an instance where my trackers shouted at her and halted her within 5 m from us. The continual shouting caused her to lose her nerve and she backed off. In this case the charge reaction was brought about by our having given her a fright when she had cubs nearby.

A prelude to a charge is often signalled by tail lashing up and down, and roaring with flattened ears. The run is slow then swift and somewhat crouched with the head held low, the tail is held erect and stiff. When faced by these signs it is very difficult to remain still and the inherent desire is to flee, but this desire carries with it the certainty of a permanent end to lion-watching.

Males more often than not 'bluff' and will take off with great haste with your only observation being that your tracker called out 'Lion'.

In all my encounters with males, they have always fled.

Wounded lions, male or female, are a totally different proposition.

If you are in charge of a party and you encounter a lioness that does not run off, instruct your group, once you have assessed her reaction, to back away slowly until out of sight. Avoid thickets and dense tall grass. Although you might be suitably armed, your chances of hitting a charging lion are remote, so discretion under these circumstances, would be the better part of valour. Don't go in, in the first place.

Keep a good fire going while camping out at night and mount a watch throughout. The Bayei of the Okavango will not camp on Chiefs Island and give those lions a wide berth at night.

There are a number of people I have met who are very casual with lions, believing they understand their behaviour. They are either fooling themselves or showing off.

Never underestimate any wild animal.

Roaring occurs in both sexes, and is used as a means of communication and territorial demarcation. As a rule, lions do not roar whilst hunting and usually only give voice after a successful kill which fills the night with deep, vibrant notes. Dawn is another period for calling, once again as a means of locating each other after hunting. The vocal calls range from a deep roar to low soft moaning coughs.

Apart from roaring, territorial avoidance is both visual and olfactory.

Lions are extremely powerful and are good jumpers and swimmers. The powerful claws are fully retractile like all true cats.

They hunt by sight and sound rather than by scent. Lionesses are the principal killers and hunting is conducted in a co-operative, intelligent manner in groups or singly. Lions are at the top of the food chain and have no natural enemies — man is their greatest threat.

Mortality in young lions up to two years is high. Fights among older members, accidents during hunting and disease in lions in poor condition account for most deaths.

One of the threats which is on the increase, is the robbing of kills by man.

Lions are still common throughout the National Parks, reserves and wild regions of southern Africa.

Lion faeces encrusted with porcupine quills

Spoor 6,5-9 cm long

Leopard
Luiperd
(Panthera pardus)

Zulu, Ndebele, Siswati, Xhosa, Shangaan, Tsonga, Venda: Ngwe, Ingwe
Herero, Ovambo: Ngwi   **Tswana, Sotho:** Nkwe, Inkwe
Lozi: Ngwe   **Yei:** Ungwe

Diet:
Carnivorous. They have an incredible diet which ranges from insects to any domestic stock and includes fish, reptiles, birds, dassies and dogs. They are partial to baboons and will venture to the topmost branches of a tree in an attempt to corner one. The impala are considered to form their principal diet in savanna and bush ecosystems where this species is common.
They are not dependent on water, but drink when it is available.

General: *See over*

Description:
Shoulder height: 70 cm
Mass: 60 to 80 kg
Gestation: 105 days.

Voice:
A coughing rasping sound.

Spoor:
Smaller and more compact than the lion. Neat round impression in soft sand or mud. Overall gait: 95 to 100 cm. Tread is very light.

Faeces:
Smaller than the lion, occasionally turns white in colour and contains a high percentage of fur.

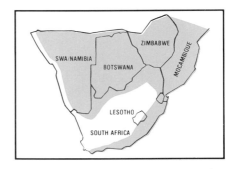

Leopards claw tree trunks as part of their territory marking.

Remains of a leopard kill in the Kalahari; small-spotted genet.

General

Leopards are shy, solitary creatures — cunning and far more silent than lion. They climb expertly and are found in a wide range of habitats from dense forest to mountains, bushveld and desert. Heavily reduced throughout its range for its pelt although probably more common than generally believed.

They live close to civilization and will, no doubt, be the last of the large Carnivora to hang on in a diminishing world of wildlife.

Leopards are more beneficial to man than is commonly accepted in that they control animals that are harmful to crops. Leopards are less easily seen on foot than any other carnivore although, on a mass basis, the most dangerous when wounded, cornered or persistently disturbed.

Never, under any circumstances, test a leopard.

They usually kill their prey by biting through the throat and nape of the neck. Large kills are hauled into the fork of trees out of the reach of lions, wild dogs, hyaenas and vultures. They begin feeding on the chest, thighs or around the anus. They lap blood readily which provides their moisture requirements.

The Impala is a favourite prey of leopard.

Actual Size

Cheetah
Jagluiperd
(Acinonyx jubatus)

Ndebele, Zulu: Ihlosi, Hlosi   **Shangaan:** Khankankha
Tswana, Sotho: Ngau   **Venda:** Dagaladzhie   **Herero:** Shitona
Ovambo: Shinga   **Siswati:** Lihlosi   **Lozi:** Linau   **Yei:** Unqaba

Diet:
Carnivorous. Preys on medium-sized antelope, guinea fowls, hares, spring-hares, porcupines, bustards, ostrich and is prone to attack domestic stock.
The prey is run down at considerable speed and often bowled over by having the hind legs knocked out from under it. Death is brought about by strangulation. The cheetah will not eat carrion or anything not freshly killed.
It is thought to be fairly independent of water, but it will drink readily when it is available.

General: *See over*

Description:
Shoulder height: 75 cm
Mass: 55 to 59 kg
Gestation: 90 to 95 days. Average litter 2 to 4

Voice:
Chirping, bird-like call, with hissing and spitting, low growls and purring.

Spoor:
Distinctive track clearly showing the claws which are non-retractile. A narrower track than that of the spotted hyaena with toes more evenly spaced.

Faeces:
Not unlike the leopard. Remains dark in colour.

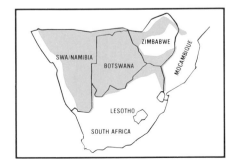

General
Diurnal and nocturnal. Records from Etosha and Kalahari confirm its nocturnal habits.
This is an animal which relies on its considerable speed over short distances of up to 400 metres. It has long legs with non-retractile claws which provide additional grip on the ground and aid swift sideways jinking movements. It has excellent sight which it uses for hunting. Because the cheetah has many natural enemies more than capable of stealing its prey, such as the lion, leopard, hyaena, wild dog and even vultures, it bolts its food.
The cheetah is not a dangerous animal to man. It can, however, be aggressive under captive conditions and it is advisable to handle them with care. A whack in the face with those long claws won't easily be forgotten.
When they are encountered on foot, it first looks long and hard in your direction and then moves off at great speed.
Mortality is high in cubs. Their numbers are surprisingly low in many areas with suitable prey, e.g. Kruger National Park. Competition from other carnivores could be a limiting factor. Cheetah are found in a wide range of habitats although they prefer open grassland and light woodland.
• An endangered species which has declined through loss of range, the insidious fur trade and shooting because of stock predation.

Spoor 4,5-5 cm long

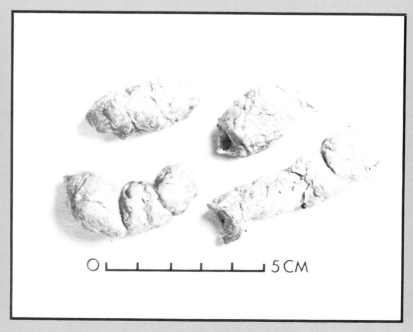

Caracal
Rooikat
(Felis caracal)

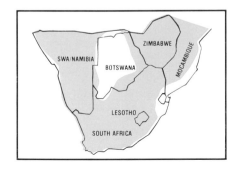

Xhosa: Nghawa   **Zulu:** Ndabushe   **Sindebele:** Ntwane
Tswana, Sotho: Thwane   **Venda:** Thwani   **Shona:** Hwang, Twana
Ndebele: Indabutshe, Intwane   **Siswati:** Indabushe
Lozi: Twani   **Yei:** Shilizabula

Diet:
Carnivorous, rats and mice are the usual diet, but other small mammals
(dassies, monkeys) and game birds are also eaten. More powerful than the
serval, therefore taking larger prey up to the size of a young kudu. Known to take
full-grown sheep and goats. The prey is usually knocked down with a sideways
slap, while the serval uses a downward slap. Known to spring into the air to seize
a low-flying bird.

General:
Like the serval the caracal is mainly nocturnal and solitary. Shy, lying up during
the day. If cornered will savagely defend itself and spit loudly, otherwise it is
silent (will sometimes purr softly). Occur widely but sparsely in most of southern
Africa, rare in populated areas.

Description:
Shoulder height: 40 cm
Mass: 16 kg
Gestation: 75 days, up to
2 kittens.

Spoor:
Similar to the serval, 4,5-5 cm
long.

Faeces:
Occasionally turns white, hair and
fine bone fragments. Fairly long
for the animal's size.

109

Spoor 4 – 4,5 cm long

O |—|—|—|—| 5 CM

Serval
Tierboskat
(Felis serval)

Xhosa: Hlosi, Ngwenkala   **Zulu, Sindebele:** Ndlozi
Siswati: Indloti   **Tswana:** Tadi   **Venda:** Didingwe
South Sotho: Qoako, Phaha, Tholi   **Shona:** Nzudzi
Ndebele: Inhlozi   **Lozi:** Nwela   **Yei:** Unqosile

Diet:
Carnivorous. Preys on game birds and small mammals such as rodents and small antelope (duiker) possible fish and vegetable matter is eaten as well. Often raids poultry.

General:
Servals are nocturnal and occur in pairs or alone. These cats are shy and retiring, hiding up during the day in reedbeds, tall grass and scrub bush. If pursued will take to a tree, climbing with ease. The plaintive 'how-how-how' cry, high-pitched, may be heard where the species is numerous. The serval is widespread and rather common throughout southern Africa, except in the drier areas of Namibia, Botswana, the Cape, Orange Free State and western Transvaal. Hunted mercilessly, now protected in the Cape.

Description:
Shoulder height: 50 cm
Mass: 10 to 19 kg
Length: 71 cm (without tail),
(tail: 27 cm)
Gestation: 75 days, 2 to 4 kittens.
Breeding: The summer months August-February.

Spoor:
Similar to the caracal 4 to 4,5 cm long.

Faeces:
Not unlike the caracal in every aspect, often contains a great deal of fur.

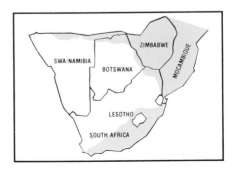

111

African Wild Cat Vaalboskat

(Felis lybica)

Shona: Nhiriri **Ndebele:** Igola **Tswana:** Phahe
Shangaan: Mphaha **Venda:** Phaha **Southern Sotho:** Tsetse
Zulu: Mpaka **Xhosa:** Ngada **Siswati:** Imbodla **Lozi:** Sinono **Yei:** Uqhumu

Diet:
Varied — poultry, rodents, birds, reptiles, insects, hares, and wild fruit.

General:
The cat of the ancient Egyptians. It is wide-spread with a wide habitat tolerance.
Nocturnal and shy, it frequents tall grass and thick bush.

Actual Size

Description:
Shoulder height: 38 cm
Mass: 5 to 6 kg
Gestation: 56 to 60 days.

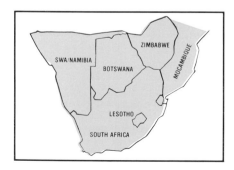

Spoor:
Similar to the domestic cat.

112

Small spotted Cat
Kleingekoldekat
(Felis nigripes)

Southern Sotho: Tsetse

Diet:
Springhares, rats, mice, ground squirrels, lizards.

General:
Little is known of this small cat which is endemic to southern Africa.

Actual Size

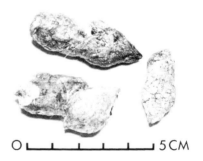

O └─┴─┴─┴─┴─┘ 5 CM

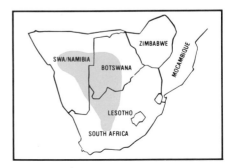

Description:
Shoulder height: 25 cm

113

Fore

Hind 8-9 cm long

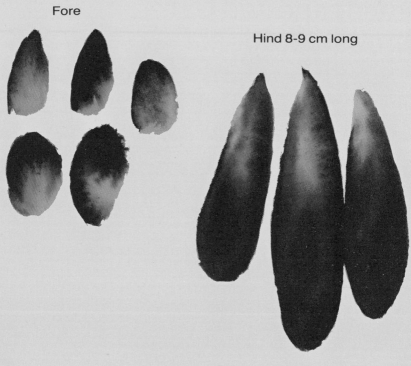

O └─┴─┴─┴─┴─┴─┘ 5 CM

Aardvark
Erdvark
(Orycteropus afer)

Shona: Sambani **Ndebele:** Isambane **Zulu:** Sambane
Shangaan: Xombana **Venda:** Thagalu **Transvaal Sotho:** Thakadu
Siswati: Sambane **Lozi:** Takalo **Yei:** Ungengu

Diet:
Almost exclusively termites; with well-developed claws it digs into termite
mounds and inserts its 45 cm long tongue to which the termites adhere.
Has been known to eat wild melons as well as ants.

General:
Nocturnal, solitary, powerful animals capable of digging at great speed.
Widespread distribution throughout southern Africa. The flesh is greatly sought
after by black people.
They dig their own burrows which ecologically are of considerable importance to
a wide variety of animals, which adopt them as homes: porcupines, pythons,
warthogs, jackals, hyaenas, leopards, wild dogs and wild cats.
Hearing and scent well-developed for sniffing and listening for their food source.
The leopard and the lion, particularly the latter, are their principal enemies.
These animals are seldom seen, but one is constantly reminded of their
presence when one's vehicle falls into a large hole whilst driving through the
bush!

Description:
Overall length: 1,5 m
Shoulder height: 60 cm
Mass: Up to 68 kg
Gestation: 210 days — single
young.

Spoor:
Up to 9 cm long, the triple
indentation is unmistakable in the
soil.

Faeces:
These distinctive oblong pellets are
almost completely made up of
sand. These animals cover their
droppings.

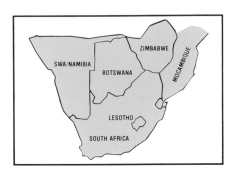

Hind

Fore

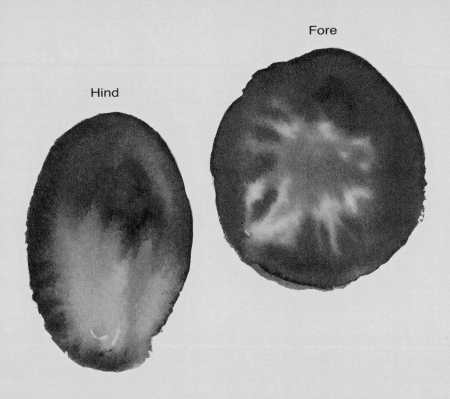

Elephant
Olifant
(*Loxodonta africana*)

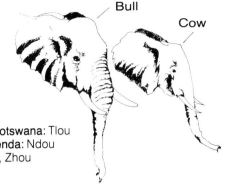
Bull
Cow

Zulu, Siswati, Xhosa: Ndhlovu
Transvaal Shangaan, Tsanga: Ndlopfu   **Motswana**: Tlou
Transvaal Sotho: Tlou   **Herero**: Ndjou   **Venda**: Ndou
Sindebele: Ndhlovu, Nkubu   **Shona**: Nzou, Zhou
Lozi: Tou   **Yei**: Unjovo

Habits:
By nature, elephants are essentially gregarious creatures and may be found in groups of 10 to 20 and up to 50 and more. Massing of elephants in numbers in excess of 100 is usually caused by outside pressures, but may also occur at certain times of the year towards the end of the dry season. Elephant behaviour, however, varies from area to area.
Elephants have a highly developed social structure and family units are led by a 'matriarch'. This cow elephant is, by natural selection, the most experienced and automatically assumes leadership. The herd composition varies and one will find bulls of various ages in attendance.
Bulls are fairly easily distinguished from cows because they have rounded foreheads, whereas that of the cow is angular.
Both sexes carry tusks. Bulls leave the family unit at puberty which is reached in 10-12 years and, in many instances, are driven out by the older cows.
Elephants breed throughout the year and a cow will produce every 5 years or so. A calf stands about 90 cm at birth and for the first year is able to walk under its mother's belly. Two mammae are situated between the forelegs and the calf suckles with its mouth until about 2 years old.

Diet:
Elephants spend between 16 and 18 hours per day eating and cover a considerable distance whilst feeding. They have a simple digestive system and require a large amount of food — adult bulls eat between 181 and 270 kg of fodder per day.

Description:
Shoulder height: 3 m
Mass: Up to 7 000 kg. At birth calves weigh about 120 kg
Gestation: 22 months.
Single calf. Twins have been recorded, but this is extremely rare.
Duration of life: 55 to 70 years.
Speed: 9 to 12 km/h. Storming at full charge, upwards of 40 km/h.

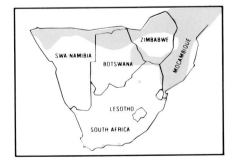

Although they are essentially grass eaters, consuming up to 80 percent grass in their daily diet, they also eat a wide variety of vegetation such as leaves, Mlala palm, which they have no difficulty in tearing out, bark, roots, wild fruit of every description and seed pods of a large selection of the *Acacia* species, which they swallow whole; the thorns of the most formidable *Acacia* present no problem. They are adept at stripping bark from trees, destroying many in the process. Rocking of seed bearing trees is common and in doing this, they open up the soil and allow many seeds to enter the ground.

Elephants are fond of crops grown by farmers and the resultant conflict usually culminates in the elephants having to be destroyed.

The animals move continuously whilst feeding and their tusks play a useful rôle in stripping and gouging bark and in digging. The forelegs are also used for digging out roots, for scuffing bark and for digging shallow water holes.

The trunk, which is a highly sensitive organ, is the elephant's lifeline being used for smelling, food gathering, drinking and as a weapon. Water is drawn up through the trunk and as much as 100 litres may be consumed during a visit to water. Elephants are dependent on water although they can go for a number of days without it. They cover great distances in their search for water and a great deal of habitat destruction is caused by injudicious placing of waterholes creating an unusually heavy impact on the surrounding vegetation. Elephants drink regularly and will go to great lengths to dig for water using both tusks and feet. The foot action is a series of kicks with the trunk playing a part in drawing mud or sand out. The water percolates through, allowing the animal to drink after the mud has settled. They will often dig next to standing water which may be stagnant since they prefer the sweeter, fresh fluid. The holes thus made by the elephant provide water for a variety of antelope, warthog, baboons, birds and invertebrates.

They are extremely fond of bathing and wallowing in water and mud.

Camps in private reserves are often the target for elephants since flowers are quite an attraction coupled with a delight in breaking down and eating aloes, which in most cases, have been brought in by the owners.

In the Kruger National Park, elephants have been observed browsing on no less than 70 different species of trees. The mopane *(Colophospermum mopane)* is one species of which elephant are particularly fond. The leaves are rich in protein and phosphorus and thus are heavily browsed.

Field Observations:

Elephants must always be approached with great caution and should be avoided unless the person has a good understanding of these animals.

Their eyesight is poor and their hearing is not acute. Whilst feeding particularly on the Mlala palm *(Hyphaene natalensis)*, they can be approached easily due to the noise they make.

I have often heard it said that elephant hunting is dangerous. This is not entirely true since an average shot will be able to kill an elephant with a fair degree of ease if he has a skilled tracker. Elephants are dangerous when wounded or when continously pursued, hunted or annoyed. Cows are normally nervous and will not hesitate to attack if they are disturbed, especially when with young. Bull elephants are far more tolerant than cows. When they do demonstrate, they put on a threat display by advancing towards one with ears held out like large sails and the head held slightly back. Once satisfied they have scared you, they invariably turn aside with back arched and tail held high. Bulls do charge, but in most cases, it is sheer bluff in order to scare one off.

There can, however, be exceptions to the rule especially with wounded or injured animals. Once, when I was leading a trail, a lone bull picked up our scent and he proceeded to search for us which caused us to retreat in as orderly a fashion as the circumstances would allow. Bulls usually can be successfully driven off by throwing sand clods or wood onto the ground in front of them or by shouting and clapping one's hands. I once had to throw my velskoen at an over-inquisitive bull, who I feared, would lift our tents off the ground. They invariably move off some distance and continue feeding.

Bulls on the fringe of breeding herds who get a fright either by smelling you or by being disturbed by running impala, wildebeest or zebra, often alarm the whole herd by running towards it. Even warthogs cause a nervous reaction, mainly among young bulls. Zebra and impala are one's biggest problem when observing elephant, because with their acute eyesight, they spot one quickly and should they happen to run towards the herd, it isn't long before they are off.

Elephants are incapable of moving on three legs and when wounded in the knee are helpless.

When approaching elephants, the wind must be checked and continuously rechecked. Move upwind and use every available piece of cover. Should an elephant stop feeding either with head up or often with the grass or branch stationary in his mouth, remain absolutely still until he resumes feeding. Move when he flaps the ears forward. Although the eyesight is reputedly bad, it is quite amazing how they can spot you and, therefore, when tracking elephants always avoid wearing white or light-coloured clothing.

I have approached elephants which I have been certain were not aware of our presence and were still in the act of feeding, when, without any warning, they have charged. These have been bulls and one would be well-advised not to think their eyesight is that poor.

Danger Signals:

A rocking motion and the swing of one foot to and fro can herald a charge. The head is also shaken with a loud slapping of the ears. An elephant charge is something you won't forget and I think Neil Murray describes it best. 'The elephant often charges to the accompaniment of a blast of high-pitched trumpeting — caused by forcibly expelling air from its trunk — which sounds like an orchestra of outraged demons. Except perhaps for the prospect of imminent hanging, there can be few situations that concentrate the mind more wonderfully.'

Elephant require vast quantities of food daily and wander great distances to satisfy their needs.

Photo: Frank Black.

Discretion is the better part of valour.

The overwhelming desire to turn and flee is the first reaction and must be weighed up with the certain fact that, should an elephant mean business, he can very easily outrun you. When infuriated, he normally attacks with the trunk held down and to the side or tucked under the chin. This is often followed by shrill screaming and sharp blasts. On occasions, no noise is made at all.

Movement is swift and one must react immediately. Little stops an elephant and although I have said he is an easy animal to hunt, he presents a difficult target head on, when charging and angry. Up steep slopes his speed is somewhat slow and remember he is capable of pushing over trees of a circumference of 127 cm.

On trail one should always have an experienced tracker who will lead you out of such situations, leaving the trail leader to bring up the rear. Do not go after elephant unless you have a good tracker and definitely one who will not outrun you all; also the trail leader must have a sound knowledge of elephants.

Sound is a most important aspect in an elephant's daily life. The most noisy instances are when the animal or animals are frightened or nervous which makes them produce high-pitched screams. This I have witnessed whilst they are in open ground or crossing a large dry river. Young bulls are often noisy whilst on the move. They produce various other sounds and the 'stomach rumblings' are, in fact, produced by vocal organs. These sounds are produced at will and they communicate them via the trunk or throat. Growling is how I would describe the sound, and because of their highly sociable nature, sounds indicate a variety of signals e.g. danger, fear and keeping in touch. Elephants use trunk and ear spreading postures as expressive behaviour in anger, suspicion, threat or curiosity.

When disturbed, they all, with one accord, remain perfectly still and silent. Many remain standing with whatever they are picking up or holding in their mouths. With no sound, the lead cow will move and the herd follows without hesitation. I would venture to suggest a telepathic system exists among elephants.

Spoor:

The spoor of an elephant is easily distinguished, the forefoot being larger than the hind foot and oval in shape. The hind foot is cylindrical and longer with four toes on each foot. The forefoot has five toes. Elephants, for all their size, walk in a narrow path with the hind foot coming up into the place of the forefoot or just behind it.

When tracking elephant in dust or on hard ground, it is a good thing to stand back and gaze down the length of the stride. This will allow you sight of the 'scuff' mark which characterises the hind foot. The forefoot is picked up, whereas the hind foot scrapes the ground. This is a good way of checking the direction in which they are heading.

The sole of the foot is like a mosaic pattern, hard, with sharp pieces of the hardened skin standing out. The animal is thus able to move over smooth surfaces and the action of movement is like a jelly baby and enables the elephant to deaden the sound of leaves and branches contracting as it lifts, flattening as it is placed down. Elephants are most cautious in muddy conditions and when the going is heavy. Babies often fall flat onto their faces and slither about. They therefore avoid low-lying muddy areas during heavy rain, preferring the high ground.

No gradient is too steep for an elephant or surface too stony. I have seen paths worn into sandstone where elephants have for years trekked up into the hills for water.

In Kaokoland their paths are like worn vehicle tracks as they follow in single file out over the desert to water. Professor Bothma recorded an elephant track in the Hoanib river in that part of the world, which was 80 cm long and 58 cm wide.

Rubbing:

Elephants are fond of rubbing and will use convenient trees or rocks for this purpose. One finds evidence of this usually by observing mud which has been scraped off on to the trees.

Elephants will dust themselves frequently after they have covered themselves in water and often when they are dry and hot. They do this by digging a hole in a favourite spot where the soil is soft and these holes are often found against a river bank.

Faeces:

The dung of elephants, when fresh, is bright olive to yellow in colour. It has a strange rather pleasant smell about it and stories of elephant hunters covering themselves in it to disguise their scent are often recounted.

A good way of testing the freshness of the dung, is to thrust your hand into the centre. If it is fresh you will feel the warmth. The colour changes as it dries and a good tracker can tell whether it was dropped today or yesterday or three days ago. When it is dark in colour and in shade it can be up to five or six hours old, thereafter it lightens. Stress factors cause a diarrhoeal action and when running the faeces will often be spread out and not in the usual ball shape. Other factors are caused by change in vegetation and seasons. For instance, during winter there is a considerable reduction in the water content in plants and, consequently, there is as much as 40 per cent less water content in the faeces of most herbivores. Animals, therefore, become more highly selective in their winter diet.

Dung beetles play a vital role and will break up the dung of an elephant in no time. Belonging to the 200 000 scarab beetle family, we have 1 800 species of Coprid dung beetles in southern Africa. Certain species stick strictly to elephant and in one pile of dung in the Kruger National Park, 7 000 beetles were found busily churning away.

Francolins are the other agent for scattering elephant dung and this they do in their search for seeds etc.

It would be as well at this point to go to the other side of the coin and take a look at the teeth of the elephant. During his lifetime, he has six sets of molars which, when worn, are replaced and pushed out from behind. The elephant's life span is governed by the life of his teeth. The tusks are upper incisors which grow out and upwards. The name *Loxodonta* refers to the enamel pattern on the surface of the molars.

When elephant numbers greatly increase the inevitable destruction of the habitat follows. Control of elephant populations in southern Africa is regularly maintained by cropping.

123

Tree Dassie
Boomdassie
(Dendrohyrax arboreus)

Siswati: Imbila ye ma hlatsi

Diet:
Vegetarian; mostly leaves.

General:
Tree dassies are nocturnal and arboreal and less gregarious than the other dassies. They occur on the Eastern seaboard in coastal and sub-coastal forest, the Eastern Transvaal, Natal Midlands and Swaziland. They live in rocky crevices and the hollows of trees. Their cry is a piercing scream. Dark brown in colour with long soft fur. Creamy-white dorsal spot.

O └─┴─┴─┴─┴─┘ 5 CM

Description:
Overall length: 50 cm
Mass: Up to 4,5 kg
Gestation: about 210 days.

Faeces:
Clustered.
Defecate and urinate on the same spot.

Spoor:
Similar to that of the rock dassie.

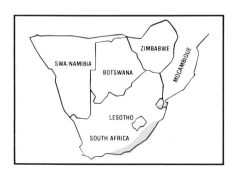

124

Rock Dassie
Klipdassie
(Procavia capensis)

Shona: Mbila   **Ndebele:** Imbila   **Zulu, Xhosa, Siswati,**
Shangaan: Mbili   **Sotho:** Pela   **Venda:** Mbila

Other English names: Rock rabbit or rock hyrax.

Diet:
Vegetarian; leaves, grass, shoots, twigs, fruits.

General:
Gregarious, diurnal, living in small and large colonies amongst koppies, hills and rocky outcrops. They have numerous enemies and rely on their senses, sight and sound. They possess excellent ability in climbing rocky slopes or trees. At the approach of danger they utter shrill barks and whistles and retreat with great haste to the safety of their rocky lairs. They are preyed upon by a variety of animals, with the leopard and black eagle high on the list. Pythons too are among their enemies. The flesh is pleasant and eaten by various tribes. They possess extremely long upper incisors which they can use most effectively and they will bite anything that attempts to molest them. Black dorsal spot.

Fore

Hind

Actual Size

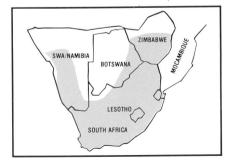

O └─┴─┴─┴─┴─┘ 5 CM

Description:
Overall length: 50 cm
Mass: Up to 4,5 kg
Gestation: 225 days.

RS

Spoor:
See yellow-spotted dassie.

Faeces:
Strong-smelling due to the urine and dark in colour, found in rock clefts and at the entrance to caves, 1 cm long.

Yellow-spotted Rock Dassie
Geelkoldassie
(Heterohyrax brucei)

Shona: Mbira   **Ndebele:** Imbila

Diet:
As for the rock dassie, including bulbs.

General:
The habitat of this smaller dassie is similar to that of the rock dassie, but with a far more restricted range. Does not occur in South Africa, other than in the Northern Transvaal. The distinguishing feature is the yellow spot situated on the back (mid-dorsally). Smaller than the rock dassie.

Fore   **Hind**

Actual Size

RS

Spoor:
The toes do not have claws but small blunt nails, with the soles naked and moistened by a gland. The second toe has a nail for grooming. The soles are so designed as to act as a suction pad, enabling them to run up near-vertical faces. Four toes on front feet, three on hind.

O └─┴─┴─┴─┴─┘ 5 CM

Faeces:
Deposit their droppings in selected latrines which are often piled fairly high.
They urinate in other spots, mainly on sloping rock. The urine is prized in South Africa for its medicinal properties, as a result of its crystallising action which forms slabs on the rock surface. It has a strong, musky odour.

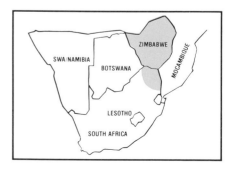

Kaokoveld Rock Dassie
Kaokoveldklipdassie
(*Procavia welwitschii*)

Diet:
Similar to the rock dassie. Browse on the foliage of stunted bushes and forbs.

General:
Confined to the Kaokoveld of Namibia and the south-western tip of Angola.

Description:
Overall length: ± 46 cm
Smaller than the rock dassie. Fur
short and coarse; dorsal spot
light-yellow.

Spoor:
As in the yellow-spotted rock
dassie and the rock dassie, the
Kaokoveld Rock dassie has
four digits on the forefeet and
three on the hind.

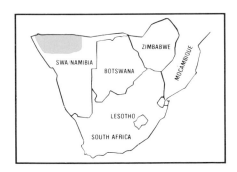

Spoor 20 – 25 cm long

Hook-lipped (Black) Rhinoceros
Swartrenoster

(Diceros bicornis)

Zulu: uBhejane   **Transvaal Sotho:** Makgale   **Xhosa:** Mkhohombe
Tswana: Tshukudu   **Venda:** Thema   **Herero:** Ngara
Kung Bushman: Khi   **Sindebele:** uBhejane
Shona: Chipenbere, Nhema   **Lozi:** Sukulu   **Yei:** Unshunguzu

Diet:
Browser, known to graze seasonally. Usually found in thickets where it eats shrubs, twigs, leaves. Thorns present no problem.

General:
Prehensile lip. Head held high. Smaller than the square-lipped rhinoceros. Hook-lipped rhinoceroses can display considerable aggression when alarmed. Normally shy. Usually solitary. Poor sight but possesses keen hearing and sense of smell. Agile. Head held horizontal in a charge – will lift the whole front portion of the body off the ground when tossing its target which could result in a most unpleasant surprise. Tail held erect on the run. Loud puffing and snorting. Calf runs behind the mother.

Description:
Shoulder height: 1,6 m
Mass: 900 to 1 000 kg
Gestation: 15 to 16 months.
There are conflicting opinions on this.
Single calf.
Speed: 45 km/h

Spoor:
Slightly more compact than that of the square-lipped rhinoceros, and smaller. See illustrations for comparison.

Faeces:
Usually defecate in middens and frequently scatter the dung with their hind legs. Easily identified by the fibrous and woody nature of the dung.

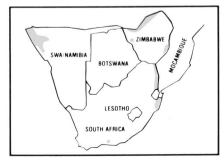

• Endangered species.

Approach elephants with caution. The light coloured shirt worn by one of these trailists is not to be recommended.

◀ Water hole dug by elephants in search of clean water.

Elephant dung. Note fibrous nature.

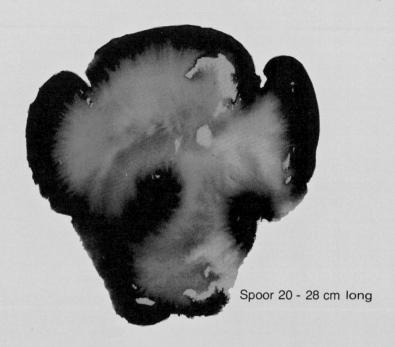

Spoor 20 - 28 cm long

Square-lipped rhino midden.

Square-lipped (White) Rhinoceros
Witrenoster *(Ceratotherium simum)*

Zulu: Mkhombe   **Tswana:** Tshukudu, Mogohu, Kgetlwa
Transvaal Sotho: Tshukudu, Mogohu   **Venda:** Tshuguly
Sindebele: Umhofu   **Shona:** Chipembere   **Siswati:** Umkhombe

Diet:
Grass eaters.

Square-lipped rhino   Hook-lipped rhino

General:
Jaw square and head carried low. Larger than the hook-lipped rhinoceros. By contrast far more placid and less prone to attack. Curious by nature. Tapping sounds draw its attention. In the event of a fast approach, get behind a tree. Eyesight poor, hearing and sense of smell acute. Tail looped over the back when on the move. Fond of mud wallows. Rubbing posts often polished to a fine surface. Calf walks in front of mother.

Description:
Shoulder height: 1,8 m
Mass: Up to 2 000 kg
Gestation: 18 months. One calf at intervals of three years.
Duration of life: 40 years.
Speed: 40 km/h short distances.

Spoor:
Three-toed – fore 28 cm long x 24 cm.
Well-used trails. Expert at negotiating steep slopes. Longer spoor than hook-lipped rhinoceros.

Faeces:
The square-lipped rhinoceros deposits its dung in large middens. The droppings are large, darkish-green when fresh, turning black with age. Resembles elephant in composition. Territorial bulls urinate backwards in a fine controlled spray. Trees and bushes are marked using the horn.

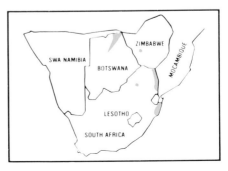

Lioness.

◀ Elephant tracks in the Shashe River.

Gemsbok.

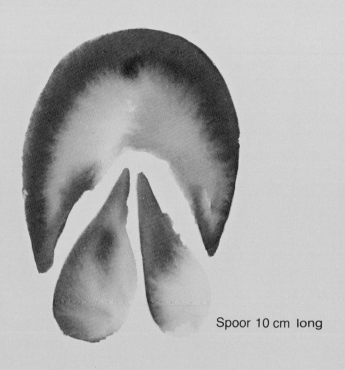

Spoor 10 cm long

Burchell's Zebra
Bontsebra
(Equus burchelli)

Zulu, Xhosa: Dube **Ndebele:** Idube
Shona: Mbizi **Shangaan:** Tsonga, Mangwe **Sotho, Tswana:** Pitsi
Siswati: Lidvubu **Lozi:** Pizi **Yei:** Umbiyi

Diet:
Zebras are grazers, but will occasionally browse. Dig for rhizomes or roots.

General:
Zebras possess good eyesight. They have a high-pitched bark, neigh and squeal. Frequently preyed upon by lion. Water dependent, they will travel many kilometres when this is lacking and when necessary will dig for water. Highly sociable, zebra herds may number from five to thirty and are often associated with blue wildebeest.

Description:
Shoulder height: 1,3 m
Mass: 227 to 325 kg
Gestation: 365 days
Number of young: One — breed throughout the year — peak August/September.
Duration of life: 30 years.

Spoor:
Distinctively shaped like a horse. A single enlarged toe. They, like the horse, possess great speed. Tip of hoof is dug into the soil when running. Poachers will sometimes walk donkeys over zebra spoor to confuse any followers.

Note donkey spoor. For comparison.

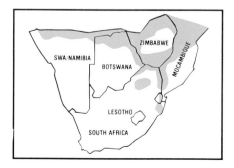

Faeces:
Not unlike warthog. Closer examination will reveal that of the zebra to be more elongated and the faeces cracks across the centre.

137

Giraffe are vulnerable to lion attack when drinking.

Elephant bull scenting.

'On trail' in the Okavango.

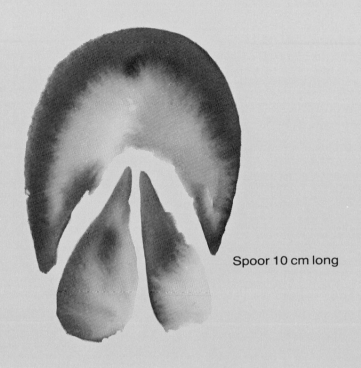

Spoor 10 cm long

Mountain Zebra
Bergsebra
(Equus zebra)

Two subspecies are recognized

(Mountain) Xhosa: Dauwa **Cape Hottentot:** Daou **Bushman:** Dou
(Hartmann) Herero: Ngorlo, Hambarundu **Nama:** Nulkhrob, Nu-gu

Diet:
Grazer. Feeds on tufted grasses.

General:
Live in arid, stony regions. Agile. The Cape mountain zebra is confined to the southern mountains of the Cape. Hartmann's mountain zebra occurs in the mountainous parts of Namibia and southern Angola. Will range well into the desert in search of new growth.

Intraspecific variation: Black stripes broader in the Cape mountain zebra which has a short mane, Hartmann zebra mane well-developed. They are capable of going without water for up to three days. When in search of water they will dig down to 1 m. Both subspecies have a well-defined dewlap below the throat. Unlike Burchell's zebra, their call is a low, plaintive neigh.

Description:
Shoulder height: 1,2 to 1,4 m
Mass: 227 to 272 kg
Gestation: 365 days.

Spoor:
Narrower and somewhat smaller than the Burchell's zebra, sharper identation. Follow well-defined trails across mountains and gravel flats.

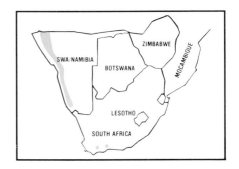

Faeces:
Similar to Burchell's zebra.

• Endangered: Cape Mountain Zebra

Black rhinoceros.

◀ Vultures often attract scavengers to a kill.

Sunset in the Kalahari.

Actual Size

0 ⊢___|___|___|___|___⊣ 5 CM

Bushpig
Bosvark
(Potamchoerus porcus)

Xhosa, Zulu: Ngulube   **Shangaan:** Khumba, Ngulube M'hlati
Tswana: Kolobe   **Sotho:** Kolobe, Sodi, Ya-thab Kolobe, Moru
Venda: Nguluvhe   **Ndebele:** Ngulugunda   **Shona:** Humba, Nguruve
Siswati: Ingulnbe ye siganga   **Lozi:** Ngili   **Yei:** Unkutula

Diet:
Roots, bulbs, seeds, fruit, grasses, carrion, reptiles, insects and birds' eggs.
Crop raiders. Will chew old bones.

General:
Nocturnal, gregarious. Dangerous adversaries with extremely sharp tusks.
Good swimmers. They are preyed on by leopard and lion. Numbers have
increased in areas where carnivors have been destroyed. Voice — soft grunting.

Description:
Shoulder height: 65 to 75 cm
Mass: 70 to 80 kg
Gestation: 120 days, 3 to 7
piglets.
Duration of life: 15 years.

Spoor:
About the same length as the
warthog, circular.

Faeces:
Being omnivorous, faeces
contain the remains of various
substances and turns dark
with age.

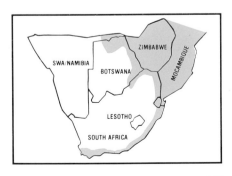

Monkey orange eaten by a vervet monkey.

◄ Baobab tree showing bark eaten by elephants.

Kudu killed by lion. Bones picked clean by vultures.

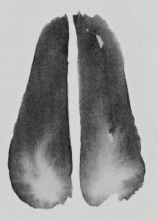

Actual size

Warthog
Vlakvark
(Phacochoerus aethiopicus)

Zulu: Ndlovudalana, Ndhlovudawana
Shangaan, Tsonga: Ngulube   **Sotho:** Kolobe   **Venda:** Phangwa
Tswana: Kolobe   **Herero:** Mbinda   **Ndebele:** Ngulube
Shona: Njiri   **Siswati:** Budzayikatana   **Lozi:** Kolobe   **Yei:** Ungili

Diet:
Grass, roots, bulbs, tubers. They will eat fruit as well although they favour short grass. Feed on their front knees.

General:
Gregarious, diurnal living in abandoned aardvark holes at night. Enter backwards as an escape and protective measure. Fond of wallowing and rubbing mud-covered bodies on stumps, rocks and trunks of trees. Their habit of rooting for grass rhizomes, is probably in many instances the start of a wallow. Sight poor with good scent and hearing. When approached will often advance towards you, only running off when certain what you are. Fall prey to lion, leopard, wild dog and cheetah. Require water daily.

Description:
Shoulder height: 72 cm
Mass: 68 to 72 kg
Gestation: 90 days, average litter
3 to 4 piglets.
Duration of life: 15 years.

Spoor:
Four toes on each foot, the lateral toes, as with the bush pig, do not touch the ground and are located higher up the leg. Length of spoor similar to bush pig, but narrower and more pointed in the front.

Typical example of a warthog rubbing spot.

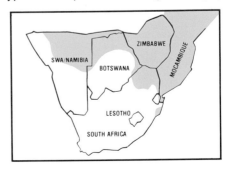

Faeces:
Round in shape, dull greenish-brown in colour. Not unlike zebra which is more elongated, and cracks across the middle.

149

Rain filled lion spoor.

◀ Young lions of the Kalahari Desert

Ostrich eggs scavenged by brown hyaena.

Spoor 25 cm long

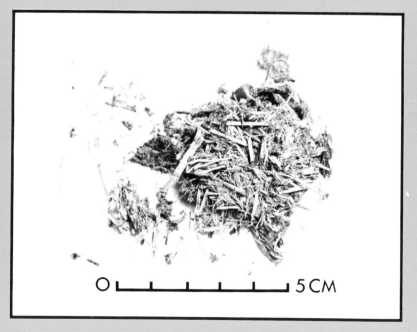

O |___|___|___|___|___| 5 CM

Hippopotamus
Seekoei
(Hippopotamus amphibius)

Xhosa, Zulu, Siswati: Mvubu **Shangaan, Tsonga:** Mpfubu
Tswana, Sotho: Kubu **Venda:** Mvuvu **Shona:** Mvuu, Ngwindi
Ndebele: Imvubu **Lozi:** Kubu **Yei:** Unvuva

Diet:
A grazer. Non-ruminating, three-chambered stomach. Eats up to 35 kg of grass in a night.

Description:
Shoulder height: 1,4 m
Mass: 1 700 to 2 000 kg
Gestation: 215 days. Mating takes place in the water. Young born on land and in the water, suckle under water.
Duration of life: 30 years.

General: See page 157.

Spoor:
Four toes. All four, both lateral and middle are equally developed in length. They make well-worn paths leading from rivers some 20 cm wide with the four-toed tracks running parallel, clearly indicating a 'middelmannetjie'.
They create channels leading from marginal swamps, providing protection for fish and opening up vegetation.

Faeces:
The dung of the hippopotamus is not unlike that of elephants who have fed on grass. On land they scatter their dung usually against a bush with a sideways wagging of the tail, not unlike a nervous elephant on the run. They also have a habit of defecating in water where the nutrients are fed upon by fish.

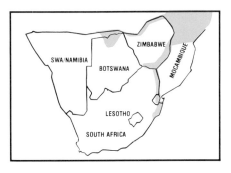

White rhinos grazing.

◀ Steenbok killed and eaten by black backed jackal.

White rhino midden (dung heap).

General:
The hippopotamus has been known to be attracted to fires. It is extreme folly to move between water and a grazing hippopotamus. Old bulls and cows can be dangerous and usually adopt a truculent attitude towards everything and anyone and many a boat has felt the brunt of venturing too near, let alone those that have been bitten in half. Runs under the water on the bottom of the river bed with speed — as fast as a man can walk. They can remain under water for up to six minutes, they swim well and in a mock charge move in a lunging fashion above the water. In a real attack they remain just below the surface.

They move some distance when feeding, uttering grunts, and will make for water with great speed when disturbed. Loud bellows when fighting. The hippopotamus is nature's natural dredge, displacing silt and sand near banks thus allowing a continual flow of water.

Canoes are sometimes the target for an angry hippopotamus and the bayei of the Okavango keep a wary eye out for them.

Impala, kudu and zebras at a waterhole.

◄ Nature's sanitary engineer; the spotted hyaena.

'Makoros' in the Okavango Delta.

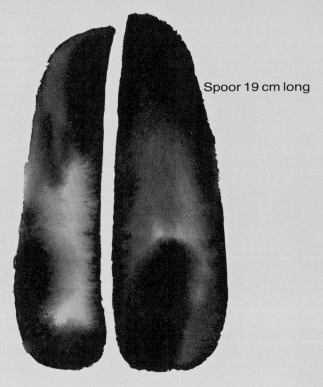

Spoor 19 cm long

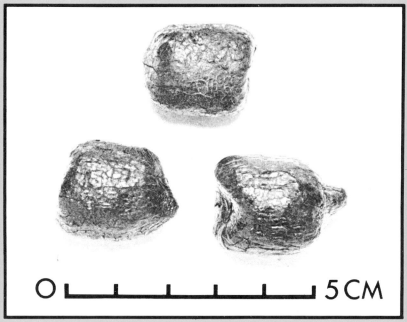

Giraffe
Kameelperd
(Giraffa camelopardalis)

Zulu: Ndhlulamithi **Shangaan:** Nthutlwa **Tswana:** Thutlwa
Sotho: Thutlwa, Thitlwa **Venda:** Thuda **Ndebele:** Htundla, Ndlulamithi
Siswati: Indlulamitsi **Lozi:** Tutwa **Yei:** Unveweshe

Diet:
A browser, known to graze seasonally in some areas.

General:
Both sexes have horns. In the cow, the horns turn inwards. They are gregarious animals with keen scent, hearing and sight. They move at speeds up to 50 km/h. They feed during the day and the night and are not dependent on water, staying for long periods in waterless areas. They are preyed upon by lion despite the fact that they can deliver a fearful kick which could easily kill a lion. The neck has seven vertebrae, as found in other mammals. They are silent animals, occasionally uttering grunts and moans.

Description:
Shoulder height: 5 to 6 m
Mass: Up to 1 270 kg
Gestation: 15 months. Breeds year round. Single calf, twins occasionally.
Duration of life: 28 years in captivity.

Spoor:
Unmistakable square-toed print. Giraffe are prone to broken limbs caused by slipping on wet surfaces.

Faeces:
Although longer in bulls, the pellets are confused at times with kudu. The pellets are flattened at one end and giraffe faeces tends to be more scattered because of the drop.

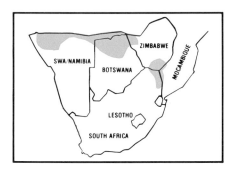

Damara Dik-dik
(Madoqua kirkii)

Herero: Thini (Shortridge)   **Ovambo:** Tingu (Shortridge)

Diet:
Browser — It appears to be independent of water.

General:
The species inhabits bush and scrub thickly strewn with rock. Found in Damaraland, Kaokoland, Etosha and southern Angola. A shy, diminutive animal usually found in pairs. It marks territories from preorbital glands. Females have no horns. Species range extends beyond southern Africa.

Actual size

Description:
Shoulder height: 35 to 40 cm
Mass: 3 to 5 kg
Gestation: 170 days.

ZIMBABWE
SWA NAMIBIA
BOTSWANA
MOCAMBIQUE
LESOTHO
SOUTH AFRICA

Spoor and faeces not collected.

162

Oribi
Oorbietjie
(Ourebia ourebi)

Zulu, Xhosa, Siswati: Wula, Iwula
Lozi: Kamunda   **Yei:** Untungu

Diet:
A grazer, dependent on water.

General:
A swift, inquisitive antelope which lies up in tall grass and is mainly found in grassland savanna. They have a peculiar gait and when alarmed utter a sharp whistle. It is distributed throughout the eastern Cape, Natal, south-eastern Transvaal, Mocambique and south-eastern Zimbabwe, and are usually found in pairs or small groups. Easily recognised by its white, short, bushy tail when running off.

Actual Size

O └─┴─┴─┴─┴─┘ 5 CM

Description:
Shoulder height: 51 to 66 cm
Average mass: 14 to 20 kg
Gestation: About 210 days.

Spoor:
3,5 cm. Pointed and fairly broad at base.

Faeces:
Often found in middens. Not unlike the grey duiker.

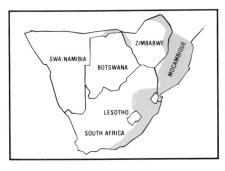

Suni
Soenie
(Livingstone's antelope)
(Neotragus moschatus)

Zulu: Nhlengane

Diet:
Browser — independent of water like the steenbok. They feed in the early morning and late evening.

General:
Small, shy secretive animals inhabiting thick, dense bush and found solitarily or in pairs. A musky scent is excreted from facial glands and they mark their territories with deposits from these glands. They are swift and are not easily observed, but have been seen in the Sihangwane forest in northern Tongaland. They are found in Zululand and north to Malawi. Second only to the blue duiker as our smallest antelope.

Actual Size

O L___L___L___L___L___L 5 CM

Description:
Shoulder height: 35 cm
Mass: 5 to 7 kg
Gestation: Little is known.

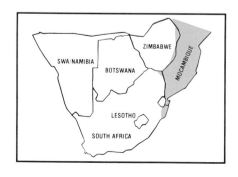

Spoor:
Similar to that of the red duiker although it is more pointed.

Faeces:
Smallest of all the antelope.

Grysbok
(Raphicerus melanotis)

Xhosa: Ngxungxu   Southern Sotho: Phuti

Diet:
They graze and browse and can go without water for long periods.

General:
They are found in the Addo and Mountain Zebra National Parks and the south-eastern Cape down to the Peninsula. During the mating season they occur in pairs, at other times singly. They are larger and stouter than Sharpe's Grysbok, and have long ears. They lie flat when threatened and prefer open grass areas often in close proximity to the base of hills. They are mainly nocturnal and lie up in tall grass during the day.

O └─┴─┴─┴─┴─┘ 5 CM

Actual Size

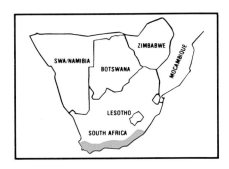

Description:
Shoulder height: 54 cm
Mass: 10 to 12 kg
Gestation: 185 days.

Horns of dead antelope are eaten away by the larvae of horn boring moths.

Sharpe's Grysbok
Sharpe se Grysbok
(Raphicerus sharpei)

Shona: Himba   **Ndebele:** Isanempa
Shangaan: Pitsipitsi   **Siswati:** Mawumbane

Diet:
Browser, occasionally feeding on young grass.

General:
Sometimes confused with the steenbok which is slightly taller; another difference being that it runs away with its head held low whereas the steenbok carries its head high. They are to be found in pairs or solitary over a wide area of the eastern escarpment, south to Swaziland and north to Zimbabwe. They will hide in disused aardvark holes when pursued.

Actual Size

Description:
Shoulder height: 40 cm
Mass: 9 kg
Gestation: 165 days — single young.

Faeces:
Deposit their droppings in middens

Spoor:
Identical to the steenbok.

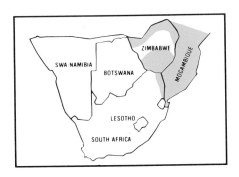

Grey Rhebok
Vaalribbok
(Pelea capreolus)

Xhosa, Zulu: Liza   **Tswana:** Lehele   **Sotho:** Letsa
Siswati: Liza

Diet:
Exclusively a grazer.

General:
A species of flat-topped, grass-covered mountains found in parties of up to 20
strong. The old males live singly.
The are distributed throughout the Cape, Lesotho, Natal, eastern Orange Free
State, Swaziland and the south-eastern Transvaal. They are not found in the
Kruger National Park, but are endemic to southern Africa.
They have good sight, hearing and sense of smell. Stevenson-Hamilton
described the voice as a sharp cough.
They show a distinctive white tail when running off.

Description:
Shoulder height: 70 to 76 cm
Mass: 18 to 23 kg
Gestation: 260 days.

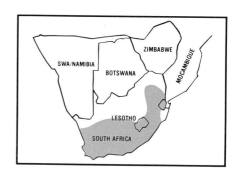

Klipspringer
(Oreotragus oreotragus)

Shona: Ngururu **Ndebele:** Igogo **Sotho:** Kome
Tswana: Kololo **Shangaan, Venda:** Ngululu
Siswati: Ligoka

Diet:
Principally a browser.

General:
A compact animal frequenting koppies, hilly and rocky country, they have a wide distribution. They are phenomenal jumpers and are able to go up vertical faces, balancing expertly on cylindrical hooves. They blend in well with their surroundings. They drink when water is available although they are independent of it. They are inquisitive animals and have definite home ranges where suitable habitat occurs. They make a short snorting sound.

Actual Size

O └──┴──┴──┴──┴──┘ 5 CM

Description:
Shoulder height: 50 to 61 cm
Mass: 15 kg
Gestation: About 210 days.

Spoor:
Their track is unlike that of any other buck, each slot consisting of two small oval pits, close together, not unlike the imprints of the tips of two fingers (Shortridge).

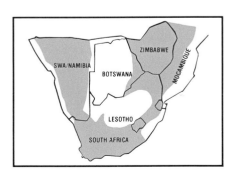

Blue Duiker
Blouduiker
(Cephalophus monticola)

Zulu: Iphiti

Diet:
A browser — leaves and fruit.

General:
The smallest of the antelope in southern Africa. They are shy and inhabit thick forest and bush from the eastern Cape, Transkei, Natal, Zululand, Swaziland into Mocambique and eastern Zimbabwe. Like the red duiker, they are well-adapted to living in forests. They drink regularly, are nocturnal and lie up during the day. They mark territories with secretions from facial glands.
They are a much poached species and are preyed upon by crowned eagles and pythons.

Actual Size

Description:
Shoulder height: 30 to 35 cm
Mass: 4 to 6 kg
Gestation: 115 to 120 days.

Spoor:
Small spoor, 2 cm long.

Faeces:
Round pellets with pointed tips.

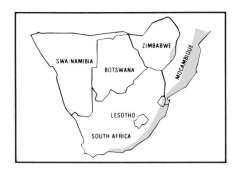

Red Duiker
Rooiduiker
(Cephalophus natalensis)

Zulu: Umsumpe   **Venda:** Phithi   **Siswati:** Umsumbi

Diet:
A browser — fruits, leaves and shoots.

General:
A compact, small antelope of dense, well-forested areas of Natal through Zululand, and Mocambique. It is mainly nocturnal, secretive and shy and is found, as a rule, singly.
Little is known about this species.

Actual Size

O └─┴─┴─┴─┴─┘ 5 CM

Description:
Shoulder height: 41 to 46 cm
Mass: 13 kg

Spoor:
Slightly longer than the blue duiker. Similar in shape.

Faeces:
More pointed than the blue duiker.

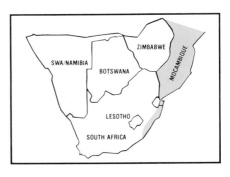

171

Common Duiker
Duiker
(Sylvicapra grimmia)

Tswana: Phute **Shona:** Mhembwe
Ndebele: Impunzi **Sotho:** Phuthi **Venda:** Nfsa
Xhosa, Zulu, Siswati: Mpunzi **Shangaan:** Mhuti
Lozi: Puti **Yei:** Unsa

Diet:
Browse mainly — fruits, leaves, grass and roots. They are fond of feeding in cultivated land.

General:
A common species found throughout southern Africa. They are mainly nocturnal, elusive and shy and keep to thick bush during the heat of the day. They are found singly or in pairs. The largest of our three duikers, they are independent of water.
The name 'duiker' is derived from the Afrikaans word meaning diver, and describes the characteristic diving action of the animal when fleeing.

Actual Size

O └─┴─┴─┴─┴─┴─┘ 5 CM

Description:
Shoulder height: 60 cm
Mass: 12 to 16 kg
Gestation: 210 days.

Spoor:
Narrow, pointed track. 3,5 cm long.

Faeces:
See photo of the three duikers for comparison.

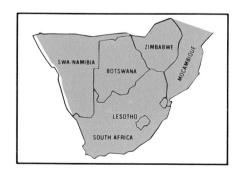

Steenbok
(Raphicerus campestris)

Tswana: Phuduhudu   **Shona:** Mhene   **Ndebele:** Ingina
Xhosa: Shabanga   **Zulu:** Qhina   **Venda:** Phuluvhulu
Shangaan: Shipene   **Sotho:** Thiane
Siswati: Lingcina   **Lozi:** Kabu   **Yei:** Ughwi

Diet:
A browser, entirely independent of water.

General:
Found throughout southern Africa. Habitat: arid and temperate regions, vleis, open bush and woodland. A swift animal which zigzags as it runs, often stopping a short way off to look back. Distinctive large ears. Fond of lying up in tall grass or under low bushes. Found in pairs during the breeding season, otherwise found singly. A diurnal and nocturnal animal.

Actual Size

O └─┴─┴─┴─┴─┴┘ 5 CM

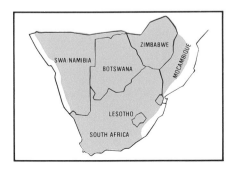

Description:
Shoulder height: 50 to 56 cm
Mass: 12 to 14 kg
Gestation: About 165 days.
         Single young.

Spoor:
Broader than the suni, 3 cm long.

173

Actual Size

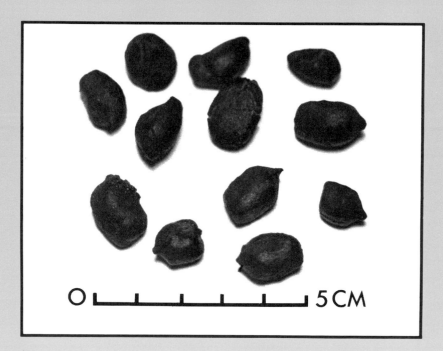

O |___|___|___|___|___| 5 CM

Blesbok
(Damaliscus dorcas phillipsi)

Tswana, Transvaal Sotho: Nônô

Diet:
Pure grazer, drinks regularly.

General:
Duller in cohtrast to the bontebok, similar in physical structure. Both sexes have horns. A subspecies of the Highveld capable of withstanding cold. Highly territorial. If disturbed, run upwind in single file.

Note: The conspicuous difference in the facial markings. Both sexes carry horns.

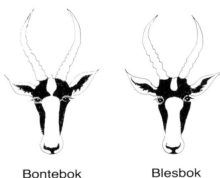

Bontebok   Blesbok

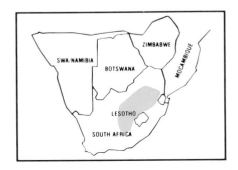

Description:
Shoulder height: 93 cm
Mass: 59 to 80 kg
Gestation: 240 days.

Spoor:
See illustration

175

Actual Size

0 |___|___|___|___|___| 5 CM

Bontebok
(Damaliscus dorcas dorcas)

Diet:
Pure grazer.

General:
Gregarious, found in small herds. Limited geographical range. Confined to the south-western Cape. Horns in both sexes. Striking appearance with distinctive blaze on the face. Swift-running. Slightly larger than the blesbok. Strongly territorial.

Description:
Shoulder height: 83 to 99 cm
Mass: 59 to 95 kg
Gestation: 240 days.

Spoor:
Slightly larger than the blesbok.

Faeces:
As for the blesbok.

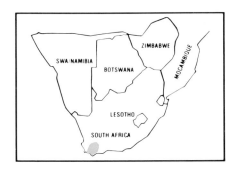

Actual Size

O |___|___|___|___|___|___| 5 CM

Reedbuck
Rietbok
(Redunca arundinum)

Xhosa: Ntlangu **Zulu:** Nxala **Shangaan:** Nhlangu **Sotho:** Lekwena
Venda: Dahvu **Shona:** Bimha **Ndebele:** Umziki
Siswati: Inhlangu **Lozi:** Mutobo **Yei:** Unvwi

Diet:
Entirely grazer.

General:
Declining in much of its range due to human predation. Will on occasions lie flat when suspicious. Utters a shrill whistle when alarmed, often heard at night. Found in swamps, grassland, vleis and reed beds. Runs with a rocking motion and will frequently stop and look back. Tail conspicuous when moving. Feeds during early morning and late evening, lying up in tall grass. In the Okavango they favour small islands in the 'melapo'. They are preyed upon by leopards, cheetahs and wild dogs. They occur singly, in pairs and in small groups of five to six. Horns found only in males. Also known as the southern reedbuck.

Description:
Shoulder height: 85 cm
Mass: 65 to 68 kg
Gestation: About 210 days.

Spoor:
Not unlike the impala, more splayed out. 6 cm long.

Faeces:
Pellets and clusters.

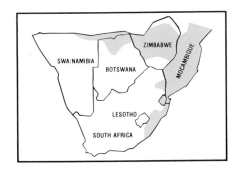

Mountain Reedbuck
Rooiribbok
(Redunca fulvorufula)

Sotho: Letlabo **Venda:** Davhu **Tswana:** Lehele
Siswati: Shitswiyo **Xhosa, Zulu:** Nxala

Diet:
Grass predominantly, but will also feed on broad leaves and small twigs.

General:
More gregarious than the reedbuck. Lives on mountainous terrain using rocks and boulders as cover. Rests in the heat of the day and comes down to drink and feed in the cool of the evening.

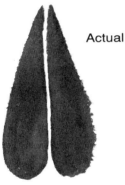

Actual Size

O └──┴──┴──┴──┴──┘ 5 CM

Description:
Shoulder height: 63 to 76 cm
Mass: 22 to 27 kg
Gestation: 210 days.

Spoor:
5 cm long. Slightly more splayed than the reedbuck.

Faeces:
Round and smaller than the reedbuck.

◀ Typical mountain reedbuck habitat.

Actual Size

Springbok
(Antidorcas marsupialis)

Herero: Menyeh **Tswana:** Tshepe, Maponye **Sotho:** Tshephe

Diet:
Browse and graze. Roots, bulbs, short grass and leaves of various bushes. Independent of water; will drink regularly when it is available.

General:
They live with equal facility in areas ranging from the dry Kalahari/Karoo habitat to the barren regions of the Namib. They have good eyesight. When on the move at speed, will bound into the air with a stiff-legged 'pronking' action, hooves bunched. Highly gregarious.
The only gazelle found south of the Zambesi.

Description:
Shoulder height: 78 to 84 cm
Mass: 36 to 50 kg
Gestation: 160 days.

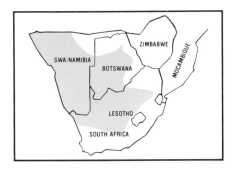

Spoor:
Similar to the impala, 5 cm long.

Faeces:
Clusters and single pellets.

183

Actual Size

Impala
Rooibok
(Aepyceros melampus)

Zulu, Siswati, Ndebele: Mpala   **Shangaan:** Mhala   **Tswana,**
Sotho, Venda: Phala   **Shona:** Mhara   **Lozi:** Pala
Yei: Umpala

Diet:
Browse and graze. They utilise a wide variety of plants and drink regularly.

General:
They have acute hearing and often frighten elephants by uttering loud snorts
when alarmed by the approach of humans. They fight a great deal during the rutting
season, uttering long drawn-out snorts. This preoccupation affects their vigilance
and you can often pass close by without their being aware of you. They are quite
capable of killing one another. They remain persistently in overgrazed areas.
They are excellent jumpers and can often be seen in the company of baboons.
Impala are preyed upon by lion, cheetah, leopard and to a great extent, the Cape
hunting dog. They often lie down in overcast, windy weather. The black tufts
above the hooves on the hind legs conceal scent glands.

Description:
Shoulder height: 91 cm
Mass: 45 to 55 kg
Gestation: 180 to 210 days.

Spoor:
Follow well-worn trails to water.
Hooves sharp, neat and pointed.
4 to 6 cm long.

Faeces:
Both pellets and clustered faeces
are found. Herds and bachelor
groups utilise middens. Often
found next to game trails and in
open areas.

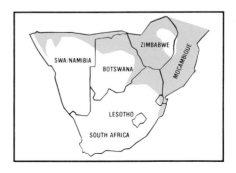

Spoor 11 - 13 cm long

Blue Wildebeest
Blouwildebees
(Connochaetes taurinus)

Ndebele, Zulu, Xhosa: Nkhonhoni   **Siswati:** Ngongoni
Sotho: Kgokong   **Venda:** Khongoini   **Shangaan:** Hongonyi
Shona: Ngongoni   **Lozi:** Kokoñu   **Yei:** Unzonzo

Diet:
A grazer. Requires water daily.

General:
Gregarious animals. Bulls are highly territorial and stake out an area similar to that of a white rhinoceros. They create numerous 'rolling grounds' often depositing their dung thereon. These rolling grounds are usually in open areas providing good visibility for approaching Carnivora. They are fond of rubbing the boss and horns on trees within their territories. Their scent forms an important part of communication. Although they are swift runners, they nevertheless provide much of the diet of lions. The voice is an abrupt, loud snort and they communicate with a loud 'kwang' nasal sound. They often associate with zebra although their sight is not as good as a zebra's. They have keen hearing and sense of smell.

Description:
Shoulder height: 1,27 to 1,30 m
Mass: 185 to 249 kg
Gestation: 224 to 250 days.

Spoor:
Broader than that of the
Red Hartebeest. 11 to 13 cm long.

Faeces:
Pellets both single and clustered.
They roll in their own dung in the
areas where they have created
rolling grounds.

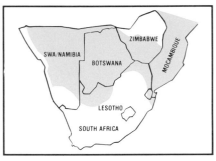

187

Actual Size

Black Wildebeest
Swartwildebees
(Connochaetes gnou)

Hottentot: Gnu

Diet:
Grazer. Will also feed on succulents and shrubs.

The name Gnu is derived from the Hottentot word referring to the sound it makes, a metallic ringing snort.
Stocky, swift cantering with head held erect. Distribution in former times extending into the Natal Drakensberg and Cape — today confined mainly to the Orange Free State. Horns in both sexes.

Description:
Shoulder height: 1,14 m
Mass: 113 – 159 kg
Gestation: 224 to 240 days.

Spoor:
Smaller than the blue wildebeest.
9 cm long.

Faeces:
Compare photograph with that
of the blue wildebeest.

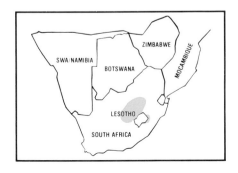

189

Actual Size

O |___|___|___|___| 5CM

Tsessebe
Basterhartbees

(Damaliscus lunatus)

Shangaan: Nondo **Tswana:** Tshesebe
Sotho: Tshentshebe **Ndebele:** Inkolomi **Shono:** Nondo
Siswati: Mzansi **Lozi:** Sebesebe **Yei:** Unsuru

Diet:
Entirely grass-eaters.

General:
Swiftest antelope in southern Africa with well-developed shoulders. They appear to have favoured stamping grounds. Some rubbing on old stumps appears to take place. They stand on anthills in order to obtain a better view. They are inquisitive creatures and will often trot towards you. Habitat change has, without doubt, contributed to their decline. Horns are found in both sexes. They are associated with zebra and wildebeest. Eyesight good. Found in the northern Kruger National Park, Mocambique, Caprivi, and the Okavango north to Chobe and Zimbabwe. Rare in the Transvaal.

Description:
Shoulder height: 1,2 m
Mass: 136 to 145 kg
Gestation: 240 days — single young.

Spoor:
Similar in length to the sable antelope, but thinner. 7 to 9 cm long.

Faeces:
More pointed than that of the roan or sable antelopes.

• Endangered in South Africa

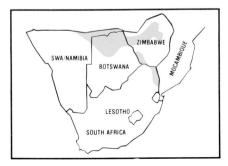

Spoor 11 – 13 cm long

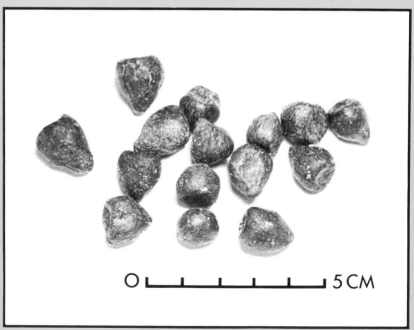

Gemsbok
(Oryx gazella)

Ndebele: Nkukhama
Tswana: Kukama
Herero: Ndumo

Diet:
Grazers. Will eat wild melons, cucumbers, bulbs and roots which are dug up by using their forefeet. They travel great distances for water although they are independent of water due to the arid nature of the terrain they usually inhabit. They are fond of mineral licks.

General:
Gregarious, sure-footed and extremely swift. Good sight. Dangerous animals when wounded and known to impale lions on their pointed horns, hence the name 'lion antelope'. Fond of rolling.
Nomadic animals often found in groups up to 40 strong. Old bulls lead solitary lives. Found in typically dry plains, desert and occasionally in savanna and Mopane woodland. Horns long and straight.

Prey to lion in the Kalahari.

Description:
Shoulder height: 1,2 m
Mass: 200 kg
Gestation: 240 to 270 days.

Spoor:
Heavy splayed track. 11 to 12 cm long.

Faeces:
Slightly rounded.

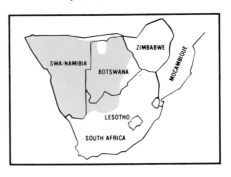

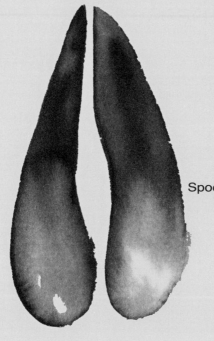

Spoor 11 – 12 cm long

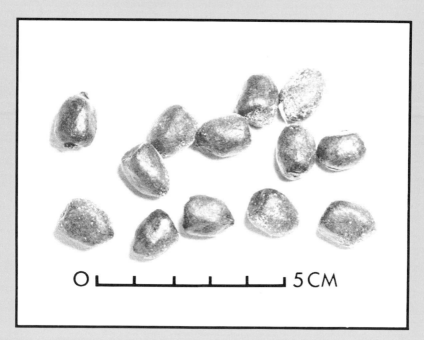

O |___|___|___|___|___| 5 CM

Red Hartebeest
Rooihartbees

(Alcelaphus buselaphus)

Xhosa: Xhama   **Zulu:** Nduluzele   **Tswana:** Kgama   **Sotho:** Thetele
Shona: Ngama   **Ndebele:** Ndluzele

Diet:
Almost entirely a grazer. Will drink regularly although capable of going for long periods without water. Believed it may derive moisture from shrubs, succulents, melons.

General:
Both sexes have horns. Fleet of foot. Preyed upon by lion, leopard, wild dog. Social animals found in herds up to 30 and more in the Kalahari.

Description:
Shoulder height: 1,20 to 1,37 m
Mass: 150 to 159 kg
Gestation: 240 days — one young.

Spoor:
Almost identical to that of the tsessebe — 11 to 12 cm long.

Faeces:
Often found beneath *Acacia* trees where they rest for long periods in the heat.

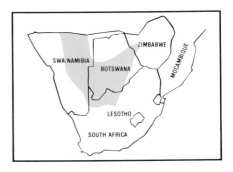

195

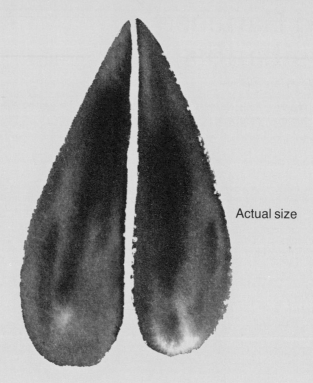

Actual size

Sable
Swartwitpens
(Hippotragus niger)

Zulu: Mpalampale   **Shangaan:** Mhalamhala   **Tswana:** Kwalata
Sotho: Phalafala   **Venda:** Phalafala   **Ndebele:** Ngwaladi, Umtshwayeli
Shona: Mharapara, Ngwarati   **Siswati:** Imphalampala   **Lozi:** Kwalata

Diet:
Grass (90 percent). Will feed on broad leaves to a certain extent.

General:
Bulls are often single or associate in small groups. Herds are usually led by a cow. Bulls are aggressive, fighting among themselves during association with cows. Hardy and tough, they will defend themselves against lions, leopards and dogs. When wounded, they lie down and defend themselves with razor-sharp horns. Both sexes have horns.
Females in mating condition, like the roan antelope, are taken out of the herd by the bulls. The young remain hidden for the first month.

Description:
Shoulder height: 1,07 to 1,37 m
Mass: 181 to 227 kg
Gestation: 270 days.

Spoor:
Slightly shorter than that of the roan antelope and more pointed.
9 cm long.

Faeces:
Well rounded.

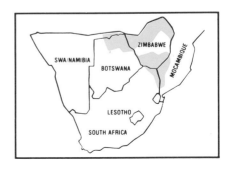

Water buck

Kudu

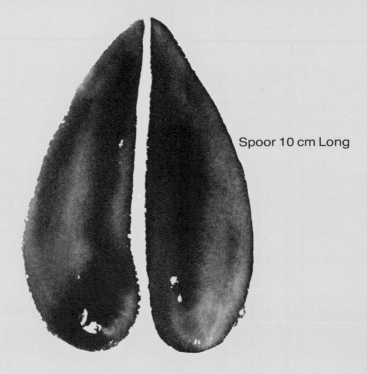

Spoor 10 cm Long

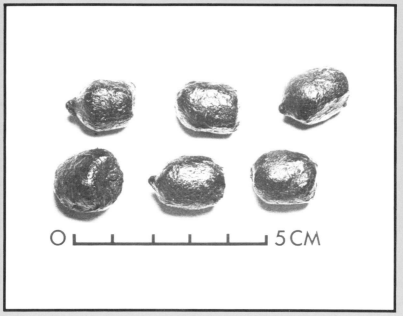

O |___|___|___|___|___| 5 CM

Roan
Bastergemsbok
(Hippotragus equinus)

Shona: Ndunguza, Chengu **Ndebele:** Ithaka
Sotho: Hlaba-ka-lela **Venda:** Thavha-nda-lila
Tswana: Kunkuru, Kwalata, Esthetha
Shangaan: Ndakadsi **Siswati:** Litagaezi
Lozi: Kwalata

Diet:
Predominantly a grazer, occasionally browses. Reliant on water. Susceptible to habitat change.

General:
Both sexes have horns. Compact, donkey-like. Small herds led by a dominant cow. Aggressive when fighting and wounded. Utters a blowing snort when surprised.
Ears long with dark brown tassel at the tips. A well-developed mane with short thick horns. Conspicuous facial markings.

Description:
Shoulder height: 1,3 to 1,5 m
Mass: 230 to 249 kg
Gestation: 270 days.

Spoor:
Heart-shaped. When moving at speed hooves spread out.
10 cm long.

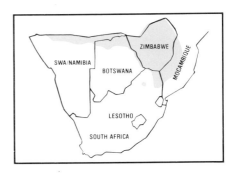

Faeces:
Similar to that of the sable antelope — see illustration.

● Endangered species

Actual Size

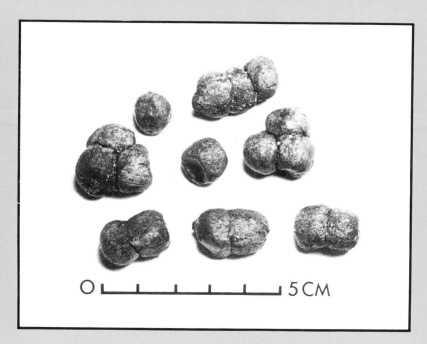

Puku
Poekoe
(Kobus vardonii)

Lozi: Mutinya   **Yei:** Mutinya

Diet:
Predominantly a grazer.

General:
They are found in the eastern Caprivi and the Chobe National Park, and occur in small herds — males are often solitary. Antelopes preferring open grassland which borders swamps, vleis and rivers, they will always be found near water. The horns are shorter than in the red lechwe and they do not have the black markings on the legs. They feed during the early morning and late evening, resting during the heat of the day. The species also occurs in Zambia, north to Tanzania.

Puku on the Chobe floodplain.

Description:
Shoulder height: 91 to 102 cm
Mass: Up to 72 kg

Spoor:
Broader than the impala and longer. 6 to 7 cm long.

Faeces:
Collected in Chobe National Park.

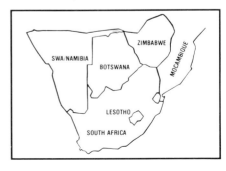

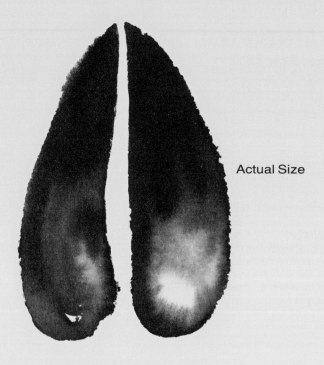

Actual Size

Waterbuck
Waterbok
(Kobus ellipsiprymnus)

Zulu, Siswati: Phiva **Tswana:** Pitlhwa **Shangaan:** Mhitlwa
Sotho: Phitlwa **Ndebele:** Isidumuka **Venda:** Phidwa
Shona: Dhumukwa **Lozi:** Ngunduma

Diet:
Predominantly a grazer.

General:
Robust, well-built animal. Small herds with a dominant bull. Preyed upon by lion and take to water readily when pursued. Bachelor herds not infrequently seen. Often found in stony, rocky areas, quite often some distance from water. Calves taken by leopard, cheetah and wild dog. They exude a heavy turpentine scent. Cows hornless.

Faeces: note comparison as described.

Description:
Shoulder height: 1,2 m
Mass: 200 to 250 kg
Gestation: About 240 days.

Spoor:
Heavy running. Distinctly heart-shaped. 7 to 9 cm long.

Faeces:
Often coagulated and in pellet form. Heavy.

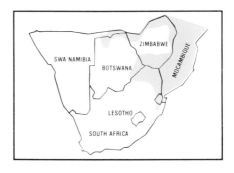

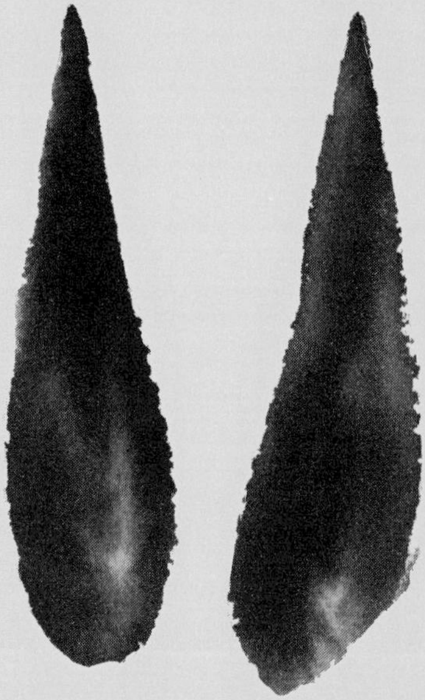

Actual Size

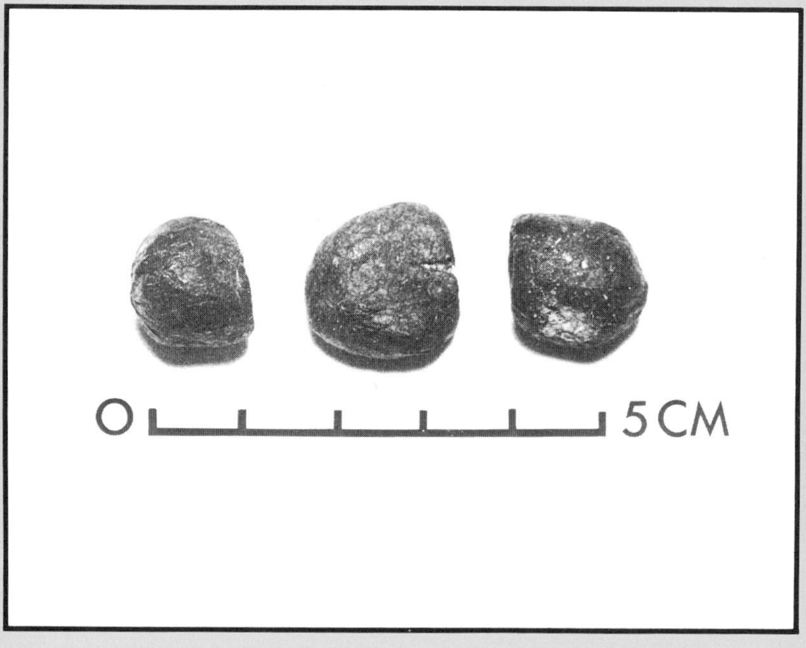

Red Lechwe
Basterwaterbok
(Kobus leche)

Tswana: Lechwee   **Lozi:** Lizwii   **Yei:** Unjya

Diet:
A grazer which also feeds on aquatic plants. Feeds in water up to 60 cm deep. They prefer flood plains under shallow water.

General:
The red lechwe is found in the Caprivi and the Okavango Swamps of Botswana. They are handsome chestnut-coloured animals and are highly gregarious. When alarmed, it bounds through the grass-covered 'melapo' with a strong splashing, horns laid back over the shoulders. They are good swimmers and have good sight, but a poor sense of smell. They are preyed upon by lion who ambush them on the small islands and edges of the 'melapo', also by leopard, wild dog and cheetah. They are not good at running on dry ground. They are also extensively hunted by the swamp-dwelling people who approach them in a 'mekoro' dugout, keeping well down below the grass height, till they are within shooting distance. Because of the hunting pressure, these animals are wary and shy.

Description:
Shoulder height: 1 m
Mass: males, 100 kg,
females 77 kg
Gestation: Between 215 and 248 days.

Typical habitat frequented by Lechwe in the Okavango Delta.

Spoor:
Up to 8 cm long and pointed. The back of the pasterns are naked as occurs in the sitatunga. Spoor slightly splayed.

Faeces:
Compact rounded pellets which are found on islands, dried out melapos in water.

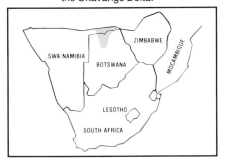

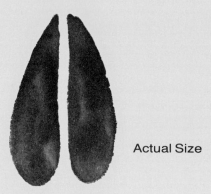

Actual Size

O╰——┴——┴——┴——┴——╯5CM

Bushbuck
Bosbok

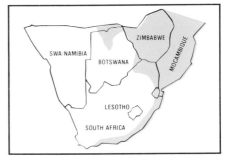

(Tragelaphus scriptus)
Sotho: Tshoso   **Ndebele, Zulu, Swazi:** Imbabala
Shona: Dsoma   **Xhosa:** Imbabala   **Shangaan:** Mbvala
Venda: Mbavhala, Tshishosho   **Lozi:** Mbabala
Yei: Ungulungu

Diet:
Seed pods, twigs, shoots, leaves, wild fruits and roots.

General:
An attractive, shy antelope of forest, riverine and dense bush. They have a wide-spread distribution, are territorial and usually found singly or in pairs. They are diurnal when undisturbed, although primarily nocturnal. They are often seen in the early morning and late evening. They have well-developed senses, jump well, are swift and are extremely aggressive when wounded. Baboons are often found in their company. The voice is a loud, sharp bark. They are preyed on by leopard, by wild dog in the Okavango Swamps and, in the Limpopo riverine vegetation, python are known to prey upon them.
The 'Chobe' bushbuck is more distinctly marked and has a long bushy tail.

Bushbuck are fond of a variety of wild fruits
and especially the fruits of the mashatu tree.

Description:
Shoulder height: 69 to 94 cm
Mass: 32 to 64 kg
Gestation: About 200 days.

Spoor:
4 to 5 cm long. Neater and smaller than the impala.

Faeces:
Single pellets and clustered.

209

Actual Size

O └─┴─┴─┴─┴─┴─┴─┴─┘ 5CM

Nyala
Njala
(Tragelaphus angasii)

Shona: Nyara   **Ndebele, Zulu, Shangaan,**
Venda: Inyala   **Siswati:** Litagayezi

Diet:
Primarily a browser, but will graze.

General:
A handsome, striking antelope inhabiting dense bush and riverine vegetation where they are not easily seen. It has a deep bark not unlike a bushbuck. It is common in the Zululand Reserves, northern Kruger National Park, south-eastern Zimbabwe and Mocambique. Males conspicuously different from females in colour and size. Shaggy coat, well-developed on the underbelly, ears large, distinctive white chevron between the eyes. Sides marked with numerous white stripes. Bushy tail. Females light in colour, without horns. Congregate in herds up to 30 strong. Solitary animals are not uncommon. Move freely by day.

Spoor and faeces of Nyala.

Description:
Shoulder height: 91 to 107 cm
Mass: 100 to 126 kg
Gestation: 252 days.

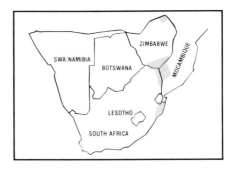

Spoor:
Similar to that of the bushbuck, somewhat longer. 5 to 6 cm long.

Faeces:
Similar to that of the bushbuck.

211

Actual Size

0 |___|___|___|___|___| 5 CM

Sitatunga
Waterkoedoe
(Tragelaphus spekei)

Tswana: Nakong   **Lozi:** Situtunga
Yei: Unzunzu

Diet:
Aquatic vegetation — they both browse and graze

General:
A shy, retiring animal of the swamps. Larger than the bushbuck with a bark similar to all the Tragelaphini. When disturbed, they immerse themselves in water with only the nose visible. They are good swimmers, diurnal and spend the greater part of the day immersed in water. They are preyed upon by lion who move from island to island.

Description:
Shoulder height: 1,0 to 1,14 m
Mass: 70 to 110 kg

Spoor:
The sitatunga has a distinctive elongated hoof which splays out enabling it to move over marsh and swamp vegetation.

Faeces:
Not unlike the impala.
Difficult to find due
to their retiring nature
and habit of spending
long periods immersed
in water.

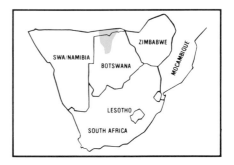

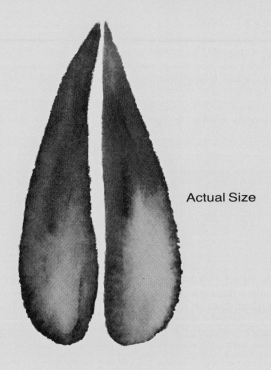

Actual Size

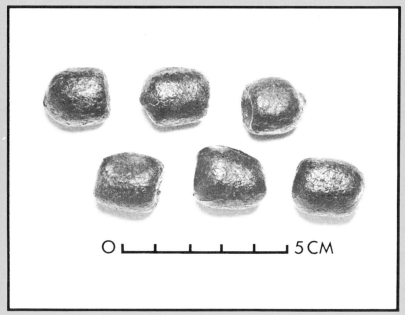

O |___|___|___|___|___| 5 CM

Kudu
Koedoe
(Tragelaphus strepsiceros)

Zulu: Mgankla **Xhosa:** Qudu **Shangaan:** Hlongo
Siswati: Shongololo **Sotho, Venda, Tswana:** Tholo
Shono: Nhoro **Ndebele:** Ibhalabhala **Lozi:** Tolo
Yei: Unzwa

Diet:
Browsers, fruit, seed pods, melons, young grass shoots, crop raiders. Fairly independent of water.

General:
Gregarious, found in herds of up to twelve. Bulls either solitary or in groups — fourteen mature bulls in a group have been observed in the Tuli Block. They are found in well-bushed regions and in hills. Shy, timid animals, they are most adept at concealment, remaining motionless for long periods when suspicious. They approach water carefully and are largely mobile at night. Their call is a loud bark and their sight, scent and hearing are excellent.

Seeds of the Marula fruit of which the flesh has been eaten by Kudu.

Description:
Shoulder height: 1,2 m
Mass: 150 to 270 kg
Gestation: About 210 days.

Spoor:
Longer and more pointed than the nyala, similar in length to the blue wildebeest, but not as splayed. 8 to 9 cm long.

Faeces:
Compact rounded pellets.
Similar to young giraffe.

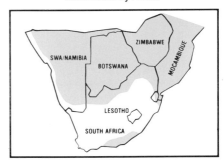

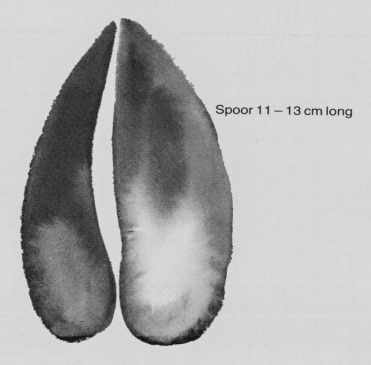

Spoor 11 – 13 cm long

0   5 CM

Eland
(Taurotragus oryx)

Zulu, Xhosa: Mpofu   **Shangaan:** Mhofu
Sotho: Phohu, Phofu   **Venda:** Phofu   **Shona:** Mhofu
Tswana: Phohu   **Ndebele:** Impofu
Siswati: Impophi   **Lozi:** Pofu   **Yei:** Unshefu

Diet:
Mainly browsing, but will graze. Fond of young grass of burnt areas. Eats leaves, wild fruits, bulbs and the bark of certain trees, particularly *Sesamothamnus lugardii* — worteldoring. The horns play a useful rôle in rendering branches accessible.

General:
Gregarious, shy, inoffensive animals. Excellent jumpers. Nomadic. Independent of water, deriving moisture intake from plants.
Horns in both sexes, often longer in the females. Inhabits savannas and open plains, dry Mopane, light woodland and montane grasslands. Old bulls are often solitary. Normally silent creatures with acute sense of smell and hearing. They are aggressive animals.

Description:
Shoulder height: 1,5 to 1,75 m
Mass: 550 kg
Gestation: 255 days, single calf.

Spoor:
Largest of the antelopes, 11 to 14 cm long. Well splayed.

Faeces:
Large well rounded pellets.

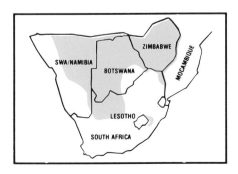

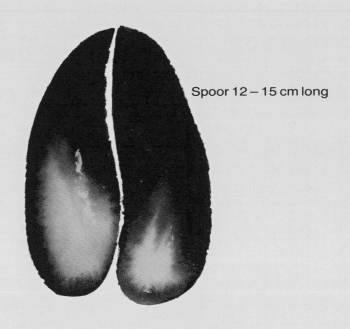

Spoor 12 – 15 cm long

Buffalo
Buffel
(Syncerus caffer)

Zulu, Xhosa: Nyathi   **Siswati:** Inyatsi   **Sotho:** Nare
Venda: Nari   **Shangaan:** Nyari   **Tswana:** Nari
Shona: Nyati   **Ndebele:** Inyathi   **Lozi:** Nali
Yei: Unyati

Diet:
Grazer, but occasionally browses on shoots, twigs and bushes. Limited in distribution by availability of water.

General:
Gregarious, shy creatures. Sight fair, hearing good to poor with a good sense of smell. When pursued and wounded they are particularly dangerous. When approached on foot, they will stare in your direction, finally running off uttering grunts. Avoid dense cover and reeds where old bulls may be lying up. Good swimmers. Fond of wallowing and using the boss and horns to smash bushes. Charge head-on and are difficult to stop at short range. They are preyed upon by lion who invariably will be found trailing large herds.

Description:
Shoulder height: 1,5 m
Mass: 600 kg
Gestation: 330 days, 1 calf.
Breeds throughout the year with peaks in August-September.

Spoor in soft sand.

Spoor:
Large, circular in shape almost identical to domestic cattle. Gait slow and ponderous.

Faeces:
Unmistakably cow-like, often loose. Dark in colour, turns whitish-brown with age. Freshness is tested by breaking open the surface with one's toes or boot.

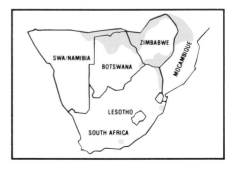

COMPARATIVE SPOOR ILLUSTRATIONS

All illustrations are of forefeet unless otherwise indicated.

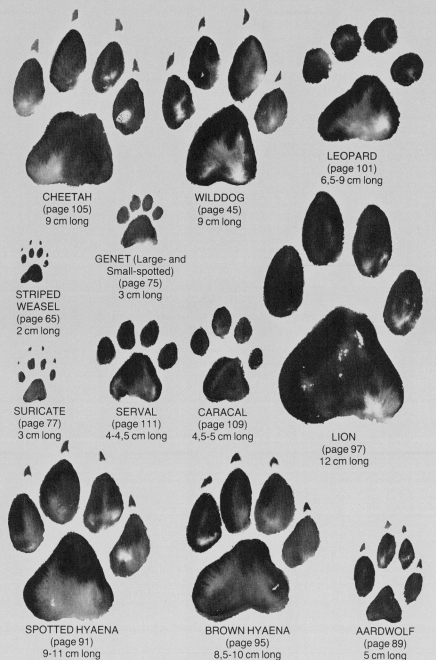

CHEETAH
(page 105)
9 cm long

WILDDOG
(page 45)
9 cm long

LEOPARD
(page 101)
6,5-9 cm long

GENET (Large- and
Small-spotted)
(page 75)
3 cm long

STRIPED
WEASEL
(page 65)
2 cm long

SURICATE
(page 77)
3 cm long

SERVAL
(page 111)
4-4,5 cm long

CARACAL
(page 109)
4,5-5 cm long

LION
(page 97)
12 cm long

SPOTTED HYAENA
(page 91)
9-11 cm long

BROWN HYAENA
(page 95)
8,5-10 cm long

AARDWOLF
(page 89)
5 cm long

All illustrations are of forefeet unless otherwise indicated.

**AFRICAN
WILD CAT**
(page 112)
3,4 cm long

**SMALL
SPOTTED CAT**
(page 113)
2,1 cm long

**DWARF
MONGOOSE**
(page 87)
2 cm long

**MELLER'S
MONGOOSE**
(page 78)
2,9 cm long

**SLENDER
MONGOOSE**
(page 85)
2,5 cm long

**SELOUS'
MONGOOSE**
(page 80)
3-5 cm long

**WATER
MONGOOSE**
(page 82)
4 cm long

**WHITE-TAILED
MONGOOSE**
(page 83)
4 cm long

**LARGE GREY
MONGOOSE**
(page 84)
4 cm long

**BANDED
MONGOOSE**
(page 86)
3,5 cm long

CAPE FOX
(page 49)
5 cm long

BAT-EARED FOX
(page 53)
3,5-4 cm long

**STRIPED
POLECAT**
(page 64)
2,5 cm long

**AFRICAN
CIVET**
(page 73)
5 cm long

**SPOTTED-NECKED
OTTER**
(Page 69)
4-4,5 cm long

HONEY BADGER
(page 67)
8 cm long

**CAPE CLAWLESS
OTTER**
(page 71)
8 cm long

**SIDE-STRIPED
JACKAL**
(page 61)
5 cm long

**BLACK-BACKED
JACKAL**
(page 57)
5 cm long

All illustrations are of forefeet unless otherwise indicated.

SUNI
(page 164)
2,5 cm long

GRYSBOK
(page 165)
2,5 cm long

SHARPE'S GRYSBOK
(page 167)
2,5 cm long

RED DUIKER (page 171)
2,4 cm long

BLUE DUIKER (page 170)
2 cm long

GREY DUIKER
(page 172)
3 cm long

ORIBI
(page 163)
3 cm long

KLIPSPRINGER
(page 169)
3 cm long

DAMARA DIK-DIK
(page 162)
2 cm long

BLESBOK
(page 175)
6 cm long

STEENBOK
(page 173)
2,6 cm long

REEDBUCK
(page 179)
6 cm long

BONTEBOK
(page 177)
7 cm long

MOUNTAIN REEDBUCK
(page 181)
4,5-5 cm long

GEMSBOK
(page 193)
11-13 cm long

BLUE WILDEBEEST
(page 187)
11 cm long

BLACK WILDEBEEST
(page 189)
9,5 cm long

TSESSEBE
(page 191)
7-9 cm long

All illustrations are of forefeet unless otherwise indicated.

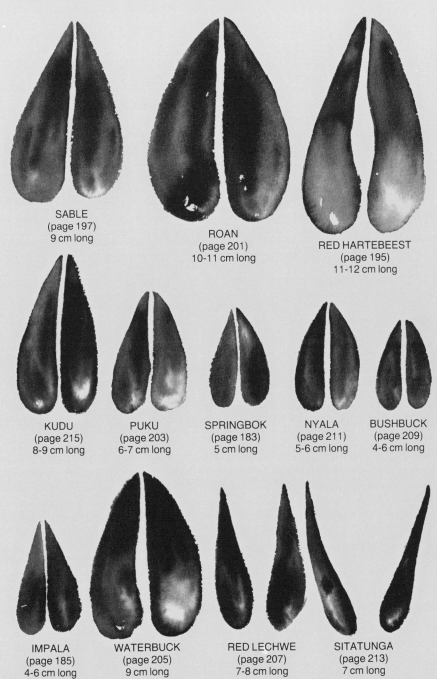

SABLE
(page 197)
9 cm long

ROAN
(page 201)
10-11 cm long

RED HARTEBEEST
(page 195)
11-12 cm long

KUDU
(page 215)
8-9 cm long

PUKU
(page 203)
6-7 cm long

SPRINGBOK
(page 183)
5 cm long

NYALA
(page 211)
5-6 cm long

BUSHBUCK
(page 209)
4-6 cm long

IMPALA
(page 185)
4-6 cm long

WATERBUCK
(page 205)
9 cm long

RED LECHWE
(page 207)
7-8 cm long

SITATUNGA
(page 213)
7 cm long

All illustrations are of forefeet unless otherwise indicated.

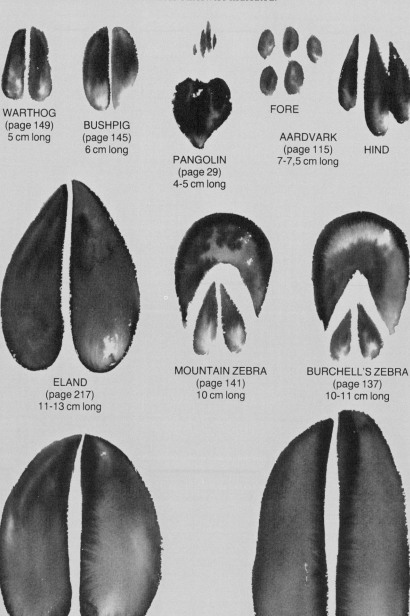

WARTHOG
(page 149)
5 cm long

BUSHPIG
(page 145)
6 cm long

PANGOLIN
(page 29)
4-5 cm long

FORE

AARDVARK
(page 115)
7-7,5 cm long

HIND

ELAND
(page 217)
11-13 cm long

MOUNTAIN ZEBRA
(page 141)
10 cm long

BURCHELL'S ZEBRA
(page 137)
10-11 cm long

BUFFALO
(page 219)
12-15 cm long

GIRAFFE
(page 161)
19 cm long

All illustrations are of forefeet unless otherwise indicated.

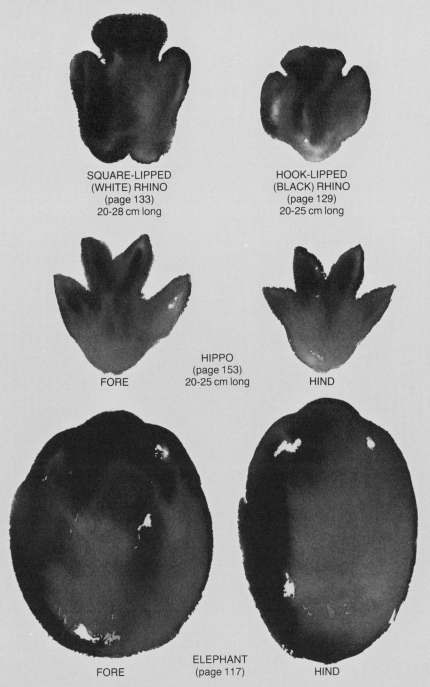

SQUARE-LIPPED
(WHITE) RHINO
(page 133)
20-28 cm long

HOOK-LIPPED
(BLACK) RHINO
(page 129)
20-25 cm long

HIPPO
(page 153)
20-25 cm long

FORE

HIND

ELEPHANT
(page 117)

FORE

HIND

All illustrations are of forefeet unless otherwise indicated.

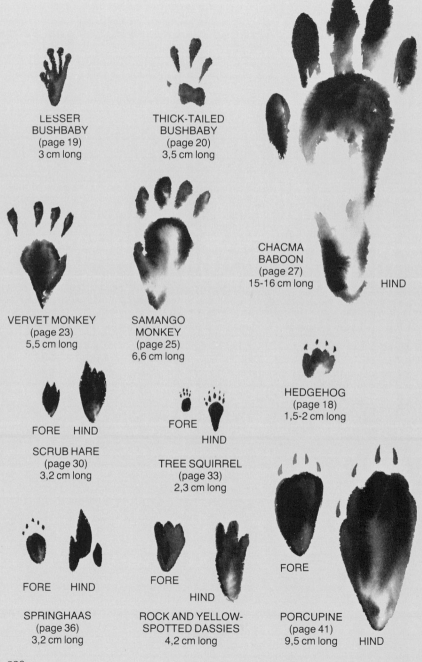

LESSER
BUSHBABY
(page 19)
3 cm long

THICK-TAILED
BUSHBABY
(page 20)
3,5 cm long

CHACMA
BABOON
(page 27)
15-16 cm long   HIND

VERVET MONKEY
(page 23)
5,5 cm long

SAMANGO
MONKEY
(page 25)
6,6 cm long

HEDGEHOG
(page 18)
1,5-2 cm long

FORE   HIND

SCRUB HARE
(page 30)
3,2 cm long

FORE

HIND

TREE SQUIRREL
(page 33)
2,3 cm long

FORE   HIND

SPRINGHAAS
(page 36)
3,2 cm long

FORE

HIND

ROCK AND YELLOW-
SPOTTED DASSIES
4,2 cm long

FORE

HIND

PORCUPINE
(page 41)
9,5 cm long   HIND

Author's Notes

The spoor illustrations are taken from field notes and sketches and from colour and black and white photographs. Unless otherwise indicated all spoor illustrations are of the fore feet. I am grateful to Dr Reay Smithers for permission to refer to certain spoor indicated by the letters R.S.

There are bound to be numerous variations due to hard or soft sand, mud and wind-blown tracks so one should not regard them as exact. Measurements were recorded wherever I encountered tracks and this one must also realize will vary. Faeces will also vary depending on season, age and diet.

The distribution maps I have compiled from my own knowledge and from various references. I appreciate that differences of opinion will arise but the maps are intended as a basic guide and not as conclusive. I have found throughout my search for references that many 'experts' differ considerably and that continuous revision is necessary and basic knowledge of mammals is an ongoing process.

I acknowledge, with appreciation, the assistance of Charles Norman for references in various species illustrations and to Bert Aurik for design and layout.

The taxonomic classification largely follows Swanepoel, Smithers and Rautenbach (1980), with some corrections by R.H.N. Smithers (personal communication).

For this new edition (1985) an additional eight pages have been included to show all the various spoor comparatively. This will enable users of this book to identify spoor at a glance by being able to compare the relative size and shape of the spoor of species that might otherwise have been confused. Where applicable, Lozi and Yei names have been included and I would like to record my thanks to Mr A. W. Bredell for his help in this regard. As a result of ongoing studies I have been able to make changes to certain spoor illustrations. And finally, a number of changes have been made to common names used in previous editions, the purpose being to achieve consistency with those names recommended by Dr Reay Smithers in his mammoth work *The Mammals of the Southern African Subregion.*

Bibliography

Astley Maberley, C.T. 1967. The Game Animals of Southern Africa. Nelson.

Dorst, J. and P. Dandelot, 1970. A Field Guide to the Larger Mammals of Africa. Collins, London.

Kenmuir, D. and R. Williams, 1975. Wild Mammals, Bundu Series, Longman Rhodesia.

Lyell, D, 1929. The Hunting and Spoor of Central African Game. Seeley, Service and Co. Limited, London.

Smithers, R.H.N. 1966. The Mammals of Rhodesia, Zambia and Malawi. Collins, London.

Smithers, R.H.N. 1984. The Mammals of the Southern African Subregion. University of Pretoria, Pretoria.

Swanepoel, P.: R.H.N. Smithers and I.L. Rautenbach 1980. A Checklist and numbering system of the extant Mammals of the Southern African subregion. Annals of the Transvaal Museum 32(7): 156–196.

Zaloumis, E.A. and R. Cross 1974. Antelope of Southern Africa. Wildlife Society.

BACK OF TRACK

Elephant spoor.

Fore

Hind

BACK OF TRACK

INDEX

Aardvark 115
Aardwolf 89
Baboon, chacma 27
Blesbok 175
Bontebok 177
Buffalo 219
Bushbaby,
  lesser 19
  thick-tailed 20
Bushbuck 209
Bushpig 145
Caracal 109
Cat,
  African wild 112
  small spotted 113
Cheetah 105
Civet, African 73
Dassie,
  Kaokoveld rock 127
  rock 125
  tree 124
  yellow-spotted rock 126
Dik-dik, Damara 162
Dog, wild 45
Duiker,
  blue 170
  common 172
  red 171
Eland 217
Elephant 117
Fox,
  bat-eared 53
  Cape 49
Gemsbok 193
Genet,
  large-spotted 75
  small-spotted 75

Giraffe 161
Grysbok, 165
  Sharpe's 167
Hare,
  Cape 31
  scrub 30
Hartebeest, red 195
Hedgehog 18
Hippopotamus 153
Honey Badger 67
Hyaena,
  brown 95
  spotted 91
Impala 185
Jackal,
  black-backed 57
  side-striped 61
Klipspringer 169
Kudu 215
Lechwe, red 207
Leopard 101
Lion 97
Mongoose,
  banded 86
  dwarf 87
  large grey 84
  Meller's 78
  Selous' 80
  slender 85
  small grey 81
  water 82
  white-tailed 83
  yellow 79
Monkey,
  samango 25
  vervet 23
Nyala 211
Oribi 163

Otter,
  Cape clawless 71
  spotted-necked 69
Pangolin 29
Polecat, striped 64
Porcupine 41
Puku 203
Rabbit, red rock 31
Rat, greater cane 37
Reedbuck, 179
  mountain 181
Rhebuck, grey 168
Rhinoceros,
  hook-lipped (black) 129
  square-lipped (white) 133
Roan antelope 201
Sable 197
Serval 111
Sitatunga 213
Springbok 183
Springhaas 36
Squirrel,
  ground 32
  tree 33
Steenbok 173
Suni 164
Suricate 77
Tsessebe 191
Warthog 149
Waterbuck 205
Weasel, striped 65
Wildebeest
  black 189
  blue 187
Zebra,
  Burchell's 137
  mountain 141

Index of Afrikaans Names

Aap,
blou- 23
Samango- 25
Aardwolf 89
Bastergemsbok 201
Basterhartbees 191
Basterwaterbok 207
Blesbok 175
Bobbejaan 27
Bontebok 177
Bosbok 209
Boskat,
tier- 111
vaal- 112
Buffel 219
Dassie,
boom- 124
geelkol- 126
Kaokoveldklip- 127
klip- 125
Dik-dik, Damara- 162
Duiker, 172
blou- 170
rooi- 171
Eland 217
Eekhoring,
boom- 33
waaierstertgrond- 32
Erdvark 115
Gemsbok 193
Grysbok 165
Sharpe se 167
Haas,
kol- 30
vlak- 31
Hartbees, rooi- 195
Hiëna, gevlekte 91
Ietermagog 29
Jagluiperd 105

Jakkals,
rooi- 57
witkwas- 61
Kameelperd 161
Kat, kleingekolde- 113
Klipspringer 169
Koedoe 215
Konyne, rooiklip- 31
Krimpvarkie 18
Kwagga, *sien* Sebra
Leeu 97
Luiperd 101
Meerkat,
rooi- 79
stokstert- 77
Muishond,
dwerg- 87
gebande 86
grootgrys- 84
Kaapse grys- 81
kleinwitstert- 80
kommetjiegat- 82
Meller se 78
rooi- 85
slang- 65
stink- 64
witstert- 83
Muskeljaatkat,
grootkol- 75
kleinkol- 75
Nagaap, 19
bos- 20
Njala 211
Olifant 117
Oorbietjie 163
Otter,
groot- 71
klein- 69
Poekoe 203

Ratel 67
Renoster,
swart- 129
wit- 133
Ribbok,
rooi- 181
vaal- 168
Rietbok 179
Rietrot,
groot- 37
Rooibok 185
Rooikat 109
Sebra,
berg- 141
bont- 137
Seekoei 153
Siwetkat 73
Soenie 164
Springbok 183
Springhaas 36
Steenbok 173
Strandjut 95
Swartwitpens 197
Vark,
bos- 145
vlak- 149
Vos,
bakoor- 53
silwer- 49
Waterbok 205
Waterkoedoe 213
Wildehond 45
Wildebees,
blou- 187
swart- 189
Ystervark 41